THESE VOLUMES ARE DEDICATED
TO THE MEN AND WOMEN
OF OUR TIME AND COUNTRY WHO BY WISE AND GENEROUS GIVING
HAVE ENCOURAGED THE SEARCH AFTER TRUTH
IN ALL DEPARTMENTS OF KNOWLEDGE

LEGAL TENDER

LEGAL TENDER

A STUDY IN ENGLISH AND AMERICAN MONETARY HISTORY

BY

S. P. BRECKINRIDGE
OF THE DEPARTMENT OF POLITICAL SCIENCE

GREENWOOD PRESS, PUBLISHERS
NEW YORK

Originally published in 1903
by the University of Chicago Press

First Greenwood Reprinting, 1969

Library of Congress Catalogue Card Number 72-75566

SBN 8371-1079-3

PRINTED IN UNITED STATES OF AMERICA

JAMES LAURENCE LAUGHLIN

PREFACE

THE following study presents the results of an investigation begun by me while a member of Professor Laughlin's seminar in political economy and carried on to completion with the benefit of his constant and generous sympathy. It has been my belief and hope that a presentation of the exercise of the legal-tender power by the English government, and an exposition of the relation between that exercise and the American method of treating the same power, would throw light upon the whole problem of legal tender and furnish a background against which an exhibition of the economic aspects of the subject would find a proper setting. This discussion is therefore purposely limited to the constitutional and legal, and does not at all approach the economic, phases of the problem.

Besides the obligation to Professor Laughlin under which I lie, it is my privilege to acknowledge my indebtedness to Professor Harry Pratt Judson and to Professor Ernst Freund, of the Department of Political Science, for kindness in reading the manuscript; to Dr. James Westfall Thompson, of the Department of History, for sympathetic help given in connection with some historical points; and to my father, for aid and counsel in this, as in every other undertaking in which I have ever engaged. Of the authorities upon which my conclusions rest, careful acknowledgment is made in the body of the text.

TABLE OF CONTENTS

LEGAL TENDER IN ENGLISH HISTORY

CHAPTER I

INTRODUCTION

THE purpose of the present study is to obtain such understanding of the origin, nature, and function of the legal-tender quality of money as may be gained from asking the three following questions and answering them as fully as may be with respect to English and American experience:

What organ of the state has exercised the power of bestowing upon money the quality of being a legal tender? With respect to what forms of money or substitutes for money has the power been exercised? What have been the reasons for such exercise?

It has been held by some writers that the power to bestow this quality upon money is a power having its origin in tyranny,[1] and corruption[2] for its purpose. That the power is one subject to abuse is patent, and that it is a power which has been abused is one of the conspicuous facts of history; yet, allowing for these objections, certain questions suggest themselves: Has the power no legitimate place in a scheme of governmental powers? When possessed, has it been so exercised as to show that it should be prohibited altogether, or is it a power whose exercise should be care-

[1] "The origin of legal tender among English-speaking people was the decree of an English king making it a penal offense to refuse the king's money after he had debased it."—Mr. EDWARD ATKINSON, "The Unit of Value in All Trade," *Engineering Magazine*, August, 1893, p. 565.

[2] "Profligate governments having until a very modern period never scrupled for the sake of robbing their creditors to confer on all other debtors a license to rob theirs by the shallow and impudent artifice of lowering the standard; that least covert of all modes of knavery, which consists in calling a shilling a pound that a debt of a hundred pounds may be cancelled by the payment of one hundred shillings."—J. S. MILL, *Principles of Political Economy*, Book III, chap. vii, § 2.

1

fully guarded? Answers to such questions can be obtained only by reference to the facts of history, by an examination of the record of what has been done, what agency has been employed, what reasons have governed action. The investigation here undertaken has for its object this reference to history and this ascertainment of the agency, mode of exercise, and reasons underlying the exercise of the power to bestow the legal-tender quality upon the money of the realm.

The idea of legal tender is a legal idea. It must be defined in legal terms. A definition which may be quoted is to the effect that "money is a legal tender when it may be used in payment of a debt."[1] And it is from a plea in defense to the action of debt that the word "tender" comes.[2] The law of tender is thus a portion of the law of contract, of the private law controlling the relation between individuals in their private capacity.

This law has, however, a close connection with the public law, in that the action of debt and plea of tender relate to the payment of money; and the authority to determine what was good and lawful money, which might be used in satisfaction of such obligation, was a sovereign power, belonging to that group of powers which, in the terms of English constitutional law, constituted the prerogative of the Crown.[3]

The definition of legal tender which has been quoted is, however, a narrow definition—too narrow for the purposes to be served by this discussion. A debt is an obligation, enforceable at law,[4] growing out of an agreement between two or more persons, to be fulfilled at a later time; in other words, an obligation involving the element of time; but to

[1] BOUVIER, *Law Dictionary*, Vol. II, pp. 24, 581.

[2] COKE, *Institutes*, Vol. II, p. 577.

[3] See ANSON, *Law and Custom of the Constitution*, Vol. II, p. 2.

[4] *American and English Encyclopedia of Law*, Vol. XXV, p. 897.

limit the discussion to money used in time transactions would exclude two great classes of transactions, the scrutiny of which, from the point of view of the medium employed in them, would greatly illumine the subject. Reference is made to cash transactions between individuals, and to transactions involving the obligation of the subject or citizen to the government. So far as possible, then, those two classes of transactions will also be included in the discussion.

In order to give the discussion the scope indicated, it will be necessary, then, to employ the words "legal tender" in an enlarged sense. Legal-tender money will therefore signify in the following pages such money as carries with its possession the right to use it in any lawful transaction, whether that transaction be a cash or a time transaction; a transaction between private individuals or between an individual and the government to which he is subject.

CHAPTER II

SKETCH OF ENGLISH CONSTITUTIONAL DEVELOPMENT

Relation of Crown to Advisory Bodies Growing Out of the Witanagemot — Establishment of Parliament and Parliamentary Rights, 1154-1377 — Aggrandizement of Crown, 1377-1602/3 — Establishment of Responsible Government and Transfer of Sovereignty to House of Commons, 1602/3-1816.

INASMUCH as the scope and mode of exercise of any one of the powers which together make up the royal authority vary with the varying relation of the Crown to the conflicting powers in the state, it is not amiss, in attempting to arrive at a proper estimate of the power of the Crown over the coinage, to review briefly the familiar course of English constitutional development during the period chosen for consideration. The period begins with the Conquest, in 1066, and ends with the year 1816. The reason for selecting as the starting-point the date 1066, or the accession of the Conqueror, is obvious; the selection of the date 1816 for the termination of the period needs a few words of explanation. The second question to be asked and answered in the inquiry relates to the forms of money on which the legal-tender quality was bestowed. It will appear that after the middle of the fourteenth century that quality was possessed with certain limitations by coins of both gold and silver, until 1774, when, by temporary legislation, the legal-tender quality of silver coins was limited. In 1816 this legislation was made permanent, and gold became the only unlimited legal tender. That date has seemed, then, a suitable and convenient one at which to close this study.

It will be remembered that in the period prior to the Conquest, the Witanagemot, or Great Council of the Nation, had a direct share in government. In connection with the

4

king it enacted laws and levied taxes for the public service, made alliances, granted the public lands, appointed officers of church and state, and served as a supreme court of justice. Toward the close of the pre-Norman period many of these powers were in fact exercised by the king; but the right of the Witan to give counsel and consent in the two matters of legislation and extraordinary taxation was always recognized.[1]

The Conquest did not interrupt the continuity of the English government. William claimed the throne by right of inheritance, not of conquest, and adopted a policy of making as few changes as possible through legislation. Under him the ancient national council occasionally met at the accustomed times and places, and perhaps retained its ancient name.[2] But the changes incident to an assumption of power by a foreign people and the harsh administration, together with the encouragement and systematization of feudal practices, particularly those connected with the tenure of land, resulted in a government which was actually, if not legally, despotic; and as the feudal influences spread and the power of the king increased, the ancient legislative assembly changed insensibly into different councils, by which the king was advised under varying circumstances.[3] These were known as the Council,[4] the Great Council,[5] the Common Council,[6] the Curia,[7] and the Barons. The exact relation

---

[1] TASWELL-LANGMEAD, *English Constitutional History* (4th ed.), pp. 37, 38.

[2] *Ibid.*, p. 71.

[3] *Ibid.*, p. 181; STUBBS, *Select Charters and Other Illustrations of English Constitutional History*, p. 14.

[4] *Concilium.* This consisted of prelates, earls, and barons, selected by the king, was the supreme court of justice, and met three times a year at the great festivals— Easter, Whitsuntide, and Christmas.— BARNETT-SMITH, *History of the English Parliament*, Vol. I, p. 46.

[5] *Concilium magnum.* This was a larger assembly of persons of rank and property assembled on extraordinary occasions.—*Ibid.*, p. 43.

[6] *Concilium commune.* This was a still more numerous body collected for more general purposes.

[7] *Curia regis.* This and the *Baronagium* were generally convened on the adjournment of the king's ordinary supreme court of justice, and were in fact the king's great court.— *Ibid.*

existing between these various councils is not known; but under Henry I. (1100–35) the Curia was organized for administrative and financial purposes, became something like a permanent committee consisting of the great officers of the king's household, and was further developed under Henry II. (1154–89). The chief aim of Henry II. is recognized to have been the consolidation and centralization of kingly power in his own hands; yet he continually called together the Great Council, and without its advice and consent he transacted no public matter of importance, enacted no law.[1]

During the earlier feudal period taxation assumed the form of a personal gift to relieve the king's wants. Under Henry II. all classes of society were brought under contribution, and the result of the nationalization of taxation was a nationalization of the protest against taxation of all without the consent of all, a protest based on the maxim of the Civil Code, "what touches all should be approved by all." This protest resulted again in the addition, under Edward I., of the representatives of the third estate to the Council, and after 1295 in their participation in legislation, with occasional interruptions, and, after the year 1341, as a separate legislative chamber.[2] During the next century and a half, and particularly during the long reign of Edward III. (1326–77), the Commons succeeded in establishing as essential principles of government three great rights: the necessity of consent of Parliament to all valid taxation; the necessity of the concurrence of both Houses of Parliament to all valid legislation;[3]

---

[1] See TASWELL-LANGMEAD, op. cit., pp. 7, 95, 97. Note clause 12 of the Great Charter: *Nullum scutagium vel auxilium ponatur in regno nostro nisi per commune Consilium regni nostri*, etc.— STUBBS, op. cit., p. 299.

[2] BARNETT-SMITH, op. cit., Vol. I, p. 199.

[3] HALLAM, *Constitutional History of England from the Accession of Henry VII. to the Death of George II.*, Vol. I, p. 19, cites statute of 1322 as the basis for this right; GREEN, *History of the English People* (N. Y., 1881), Vol. I, p. 414.

the right of the Commons to inquire into and amend the abuses of administration.[1]

This period coincides with that during which a money economy, as contrasted with the mediæval system of barter, was established, as the division of employments which had existed to a considerable degree in the eleventh century was extended,[2] the great trading companies developed,[3] the lords of the manors found it more profitable and convenient to accept money payments in place of the ancient services, and the tenants gladly relieved themselves of the personal performance of services. This transformation was not completed, however, before the middle of the fifteenth century.[4]

During the fifteenth century (1399–1485) Parliament, under the Lancastrian kings,[5] was busy in the consolidation and regulation of the results of former contests with the Crown, rather than in acquiring new fundamental rights. The old rights it continued to exercise with slight opposition, voting taxes, appropriating supplies conditioned on redress of grievances, sharing in legislation, etc.; and during this period the internal constitution of Parliament, its chief forms of procedure and essential privileges, were established.[6] Then came the political reaction of the sixteenth century.[7] Men then turned their thoughts to commerce, learning, religion, and left to princes the powers of the state. There were peculiar reasons for the existence of this condition in England besides those prevailing universally. They

---

[1] STUBBS, *op. cit.*, pp. 49, 50.

[2] CUNNINGHAM, *The Growth of English Industry and Commerce During the Early and Middle Ages* (3d ed.), p. 128.

[3] *Ibid.*, p. 342.

[4] TASWELL-LANGMEAD, *op. cit.*, p. 313; CUNNINGHAM, *op. cit.*, pp. 241 ff.; POLLOCK AND MAITLAND, *History of the English Law before the Time of Edward I.*, Vol. II, p. 150.

[5] Henry IV. (1399–1412); Henry V. (1412–22); Henry VI. (1422–60); Edward IV. (1460–83); Edward V. (1483); Richard III. (1483–85).

[6] TASWELL-LANGMEAD, *op. cit.*, pp. 323–34.

[7] 1483–1603.

were to be found in the destruction during the Wars of the Roses of the old nobility who had led the struggle for liberty, and the lack on the part of the Commons of that sense of importance and self-reliance which was developed adequately only under the successors of Elizabeth.[1] During this century the power of the Crown increased to dangerous proportions, but it was generally exercised with scrupulous regard for constitutional and judicial forms;[2] and, in spite of the fact that arbitrary practices prevailed and the spirit of the constitution was often violated, the constitution remained, in theory, at least, always intact.[3]

The death of Elizabeth ushered in the doctrine of the divine right and absolute power of kings promulgated by James and openly espoused by the church, the court, and the judicial bench as a true principle of religion and policy.[4] But during the period just closed, amidst the political inertia of the people, a real transfer of power had taken place. With the growth in commercial wealth of the middle classes feudalism had died out; and the Commons, as the representatives of the class now ready to become dominant, were prepared to rescue their ancient liberties and carry on the struggle which was to result in the execution of one king, the deposition of a second, and the installation of a third on terms of agreement constituting a veritable compact with the people. Of the conflict of the seventeenth century and its result it is unnecessary to speak. The Commons won the victory for political supremacy, and the Crown became only the executive branch of a government conducted through ministers and according to statutes.[5]

---

[1] TASWELL-LANGMEAD, *op. cit.*, p. 380.

[2] For example, Henry VIII. obtained an act giving his proclamation the force of law, " *that the king should not be driven to extend his royal supremacy.*"— 31 Henry VIII., chap. 8, cited by HALLAM, *op. cit.*, Vol. I, p. 49.

[3] TASWELL-LANGMEAD, *op. cit.*, p. 503.   [4] *Ibid.*, p. 510.

[5] MURDOCK, *Parliamentary Reform*, p. 21.

CHAPTER III

THE POWER OVER THE COINAGE A PART OF THE ROYAL PREROGATIVE

Source of the Power — Unquestioned in the Crown, 1066–1311 — Parliament Attempts to Assume, 1311–1485 — Parliament Confirms the Power of the Crown, 1485–1695 — Surrender by the Crown, Ancient Forms being Retained, 1695–1816.

THE power over the coinage was from pre-Norman times a part of the royal prerogative.[1] It was such a power as that over the public peace.[2] Thus, when Henry II. came to the throne after the anarchical reign of Stephen (1154), his programme for the restoration of order included the maintenance of the general security, the strengthening of commerce, and the striking of a uniform coinage.[3]

To so unlimited an extent had the right been secured by the feudal princes on the continent that the Norman lords had imposed upon their people a triennial contribution under the name of *le fouage* in consideration of renouncing their right to change, that is, to call in and recoin for the sake of profit, the money of the land;[4] and an effort (which was, however, unsuccessful) was made by the Conqueror, or by his son, to introduce into England a similar tax, under the name of *moneyage*.[5] The attempt exhibits the conception of the royal power held by the early Norman monarchs.

Of course the power did not remain in the hands of the Crown without efforts on the part of Parliament to assume or

---

[1] For the Roman theory concerning this power, see MOMMSEN, *History of Rome*, Vol. I, p. 173.

[2] STUBBS, *Constitutional History of England in its Origin and Development*, (5th ed.), Vol. I, p. 331.

[3] *Ibid.*, p. 361.

[4] ASHLEY, *Introduction to English Economic History and Theory*, p. 168.

[5] LIVERPOOL, *Coins of the Realm*, p. 121.

at least to limit it. For example, about 1311, during the regency of the Lords Ordainers, such an attempt was made. The Barons[1] then enacted an ordinance to which the temporary governors of the kingdom[2] gave their consent, to the effect that no change should be made in the money of the realm without the consent of the Barons in Parliament.[3] This was, however, revoked ten years later by the king and the attempt failed.

Several times during the reign of Edward III. (1326–77) Parliament was consulted on matters affecting the coinage. A few illustrations may be given. In 1331 (5 Edward III.) the state of the money was brought before Parliament and it was agreed that the chancellor and treasurer and such of the king's Council as they should think proper to call to them, and others also of experience in mint affairs, should ordain whatever they might think would tend to the advantage of the king and his subjects. Again, in 1335 a statute was enacted in compliance with a petition from the Commons, providing that no money should be taken from the realm.[4]

An interesting petition of the Commons presented in 1346 throws light on the relations then existing between the Crown and Parliament. It contained three requests relating to the money of the realm. The first request related to penalties for exporting good money and importing bad money, and was partly granted by the king. The second asked that money should be more frequently coined and that the mints should be open in all the places where they had been accustomed to be. This also was granted. The

---

[1] See above, p. 5, note 7.

[2] The Lords Ordainers were appointed by Parliament in 1310 to administer the kingdom, because of certain abuses of the king.—GREEN, *op. cit.*, Vol. I, p. 384.

[3] RUDING, *Annals of the Coinage of Britain*, Vol. I, p. 400.

[4] *Ibid.*, p. 404.

third request consisted of two parts. The first part, that the king's receivers "should take of the people in every place both gold and silver at the same rate at which the people were obliged to receive them," was granted; but the second part, that no change in the money of gold and silver should be made without the consent of Parliament, was considered an attempt to invade the royal prerogative, and to it answer was made that the king and his nobles would ordain as they should see fit.[1]

In 1351 was enacted a statute which is interpreted by Blackstone as throwing doubt upon the extent of the royal power. This statute provided that the money of gold and silver then current should not be impaired in weight or in alloy; but "as soon as a good way might be found should be put in the ancient state as in the sterling." Blackstone says: "When a given weight of gold or silver is of a given fineness, it is then of the true standard called esterling or sterling metal . . . . ; and of this esterling or sterling metal all the coin of the kingdom must be made, by the statute of 25 Edward III., chap. 13. So that the king's prerogative seemeth not to extend to the debasing or enhancing below or above the sterling value."[2]

The commentator puts upon the prerogative a construction, based upon the statute cited, which suggests the legal-tender controversy in the United States, and tries to confine that power legally within the limits which public morality would dictate; and he was fortunate in finding a statute the text of which sustained his view. But his interpretation cannot be accepted. The saving clause "as soon as a good way might be found" left the whole matter in the discretion of the executive, as is proven by the fact that two years later the Commons again petitioned that the esterling

[1] *Ibid.*, p. 430.

[2] BLACKSTONE, *Commentaries on the Laws of England*, Vol. I, chap. 7, p. 276.

(penny) might be restored to its ancient value, and that it should be provided that this should not be impaired until such alteration took place.[1]

The interpretation put upon the law by the great commentator is interesting even if not correct. As Sir Matthew Hale says of the power of the Crown to debase and enhance the value of coins without the consent of Parliament, *fieri non debet, sed factum valet.*[2]

Parliament was too helpless during this and the following reign[3] to claim for itself the power under consideration and justify that claim. This is evidenced by numerous petitions[4] concerning grievances connected with the coinage and ordinances similar to that discussed by Blackstone and similarly futile.

In 1414,[5] however, a new method of attack was employed. Parliament then acknowledged the prerogative within certain limits, but claimed the right to confirm royal acts. It was then enacted that the king should apply to the existing grievances such remedy as he should think most profitable for himself and his people, and his provision for the betterment of the money of the realm should remain in force until the next Parliament; if then approved, it should be established to endure forever.[6]

This claim on the part of Parliament was followed by a

[1] RUDING, *op. cit.*, Vol. I, p. 440.

[2] HALE, *Pleas of the Crown*, Vol. I, pp. 192–5. It is interesting to note that this argument advanced by Blackstone had been suggested by Coke, and it was in reply to Coke that the argument of Sir Matthew Hale was directed. Blackstone does not, however, make reference to Hale's comment on Coke. It should also be said that when Blackstone wrote (1765) the development of commercial interests had brought in its train not only a growth of public morality, as the interests of government were seen to be identified with the interests of the wealth-producing classes, but also a clearer understanding of the principles which should govern the policy of the state with respect to the money of the realm. The effect of the increase and organization of the public debt on the attitude of government toward the money of the realm opens up a field for investigation and speculation which cannot be gone into here.

[3] Henry V. (1399–1412).   [4] See below, chap. v.

[5] 2 Henry V.   [6] RUDING, *op. cit.*, Vol. I, p. 497.

succession of acts more or less similar,[1] and the frequent
petitions of the Commons were more heeded;[2] but in the
reactionary period of the reign of Henry VII.[3] all that may
have been gained was abandoned, when it was declared by
Parliament that all coins issuing from the royal mints and
bearing the royal stamp should be accepted of all within the
realm at the rate at which they were issued.[4] By this act the
royal power over the coinage was fully admitted and confirmed. Nor did any change take place either in law or in
practice during the two following centuries, during which
occurred the excesses of Henry VIII.[5] and the variable policy
of Elizabeth[6] in connection with the coin of the realm. Even
during the contest of the Commons with the first Charles,
although control over the coinage was actually assumed by
the Commons, the state of the law was evidenced by the fact
that no coin was issued during the lifetime of the king without the royal superscription and image.[7] Only after that
body had been established as the sole ruling power was
money appointed to be coined with the style and by the
authority of the Commons.[8]

Such were the relations of the Crown to Parliament until
the revolution of 1688. As evidence of the change which
was then produced may be cited the speech from the throne
in 1695, when William of Orange, finding himself beset

---

[1] Compare Ruding, *op. cit.*, Vol. I, pp. 483, 489, for previous petitions.

[2] *Ibid.*, Vol. I, pp. 502, 511; Vol. II, pp. 8, 18.   [3] 1485-1509.

[4] Ruding, *op. cit.*, Vol. II, p. 59. The act is cited as 19 Henry VII., c. 5. See
also 5 and 6 Edw. VI., c. 19. Ruding, *op. cit.*, Vol. II, p. 118.

[5] See below, p. 40.   [6] See below, p. 42.   [7] Ruding, *op. cit.*, Vol. II, p. 286.

[8] It is unnecessary to point out that an act of the Crown now is an act of the
ministry; that is, virtually of a majority of the House of Commons. "This was certainly a question [to remedy the defects of the silver coinage] upon which the crown
by its prerogative had a peculiar right to decide, but when the matter is of so much
importance, and so directly and immediately connected with the interests of all
classes of the community, no ministry would be disposed to give advice to the crown
of the proper mode of proceeding without submitting that advice to the consideration of Parliament."—Lord Liverpool, May 30, 1816, Hansard, *Parliamentary
Debates*, First Series, Vol. XXXIV, p. 911.

with the problems of a foreign war and of a domestic situation of extreme difficulty, was glad to throw the responsibility of the great recoinage of that year upon his Parliament. "I must likewise," said the speech from the throne, "take notice of a great difficulty we lie under at this time by reason of the ill state of the coin, the redress of which may perhaps prove a further charge to the nation; but this is a matter of so general concern and of so great importance that I have thought it fit to leave it entirely to my Parliament."[1]

Having discussed the source of the coinage power, its content and the mode of exercising it should be presented. As to the content, the power included the determination of weight, alloy, and denominative value of *new* coin; the alteration[2] of coin *already in use;* and the legitimation of *foreign coin.*[3]

The method in which this power was exercised was by a royal proclamation, or by an indenture entered into between the king and the master of the mint, in which a clause was inserted declaring the value at which the coins should pass.[4] This latter method, though less formal, was as legal whenever it was possible to employ it, as was shown in the decision of the court (1702) in the case of Dixon v. Willows,[5] when it was said of certain gold coins whose authentication rested only on indenture—"though there is no act of parliament or

---

[1] King's Speech, November 26, 1695, *Commons Journal*, Vol. XV, p. 339. The precedent then established is still observed. The Lords and Commons considered the subject separately and adopted resolutions, which were made known in an address to the king and constituted the substance of a proclamation.—See COBBETT, *Parliamentary History*, Vol. V, p. 967; Vol. VII, p. 524; also HANSARD, *Parliamentary Debates*, Vol. XXXIV, p. 946.

[2] This extended to taking away the currency of, that is, "crying down," coin in use.

[3] HALE, *Pleas of the Crown*, Vol. I, p. 188; RUDING, *op. cit.*, Vol. I, p. 4.

[4] *Ibid.*, pp. 57, 370, 458; LIVERPOOL, *op. cit.*, p. 23.

[5] 3 SALKELD (English Reports), 238. This method, by indenture, was obviously inapplicable in connection with foreign coins, or domestic coins already in circulation.

order of state for these guineas, yet being coined at the mint, and having the king's insignia upon them, they are lawful money at the value they were entered at the mint."

Summing up the results of the foregoing pages, it may be said that the legitimacy of currency, or lawfulness of English money and its denomination or value, rested upon an act of the Crown which assumed the form of a proclamation or indenture between the king and the master of the mint. If it can be shown that the legal-tender quality inhered in all lawful money, it would follow that in the acts of the Crown regulating the money could be traced the legal-tender policy of the English government. In the following chapter an attempt will be made to show that such was the fact.

CHAPTER IV

ALL LAWFUL MONEY A LEGAL TENDER

English and American Forms of Legislation Contrasted — Distinction Between Cash and Time Transactions — Cash Transactions — Transactions with King's Officers — Time Transactions.

BY the constitution of the United States two distinct prohibitions are laid upon the states: " No state shall coin money ; . . . . make anything but gold and silver coin a legal tender in payment of debts."[1] By the act of April 2, 1792,[2] establishing a mint and regulating the coin of the United States, it was expressly provided[3] that "all gold and silver coins which shall have been struck at and issued from said mint shall be a lawful tender in all payments whatsoever." That is, under our American legislation, the legal-tender quality is a power expressly conferred upon certain forms of money, while withheld from other forms, or perhaps conferred to a limited extent upon others. Such express bestowal of this power was not, however, essential under the English law, but the quality of being a " tender in payment of debts" inhered in all lawful money. " Currency," being " current coin," meant coin or money which was full legal tender unless the contrary was expressed. If the coin was not to be an unlimited legal tender, current in respect to all transactions, whatever the amount involved, and to all persons, the limitation was clearly stated.

Money transactions readily divide themselves into such as are begun and completed at one and the same time, in which, as in bargain and sale, money passes for goods ; and those in which a period of time elapses between the date on

[1] Constitution of the United States, I, 10, 1.
[2] *United States Statutes at Large*, Vol. I, p. 246.   [3] *Ibid.*, Sec. 16.

which an agreement is made and that on which that agreement is fulfilled.   For these two classes the familiar terms "executed" and "executory" contracts may be accepted.

In considering this class of contracts it should be borne in mind that in the early portion of the period under consideration freedom of contract and of commerce did not exist in England in the sense in which we understand these terms.   Government monopolized[1] the function of coinage and enforced its monopoly by imposing penalties for the offense of refusing the king's coins at the values set upon them by the king, and by prohibiting the currency of coins whose circulation would interfere with the coins issued from the king's mints.[2]   This legislation had its counterpart, of course, in other legislation regulating prices,[3] so that as the value of the coin went down the price charged for goods might, if possible, be kept from going up.

It should also be borne in mind that in discussing so long a period as the one under consideration words employed may have different signification where applied to different divisions of the period.   For example, at the time of the Conquest, and for a considerable period thereafter,[4] payments were often made by weight instead of by tale. The extent of this practice cannot be stated; but such a practice would obviously have an effect on legislation proclaiming certain money current at stated rates.

[1] ASHLEY, *op. cit.*, p. 175.

[2] For example, by the Statute of the Staple, in 1353 (27 Edward III.), it was provided that if any person wished to receive good money of gold or silver in payment, other than the king's money, he should be allowed to do so: but no one should be compelled to take such money against his will.   This was repeated in 1367 (41 Edward III.) because of light foreign money which has been imported.—RUDING, *op. cit.*, Vol. I, p. 440.

[3] See p. 40, for illustration.

[4] For discussion of extent and duration of this practice, see CUNNINGHAM, *Growth of English Industry and Commerce During the Early and Middle Ages*, p. 326, note 5.   See also MADOX, *History of the Exchequer*, Vol. I, chap. ix, for forms of payment to treasury in early times.

In ascertaining the relations which existed between coins of the two metals in executed contracts, the history of the first issue of gold coins will prove instructive. When, in 1257, Henry III. tried to introduce gold into the English currency, he issued pennies of fine gold, each weighing as much as two silver pennies, $\frac{1}{120}$ of a tower pound, and ordered that each of them should pass at the value of twenty silver pennies. "A writ issued commanding the mayor of London to proclaim in that city that the gold money which the king had caused to be made should be immediately[1] current there and elsewhere within the realm of England in all transactions of buying and selling at the rate of twenty pennies of sterlings for every gold penny; and that the king's money of silver should be current as it had been before."[2] Here is an illustration of an early exercise of the legal-tender power. The issue of gold pennies[3] was unfavorably received, and protest was made by the citizens of London, whereupon a second proclamation issued[4] declaring that no one should be obliged to receive the gold coins; and those who had taken them might bring them to the royal exchange and there receive the value for which they had been made current.[5]

Again, in the early time,[6] the penny was the only silver coin struck, and it was provided that, "on account of the poor, whenever necessity required the penny might be divided into half-pennies and farthings." On complaint that the fractional pieces resulting from this crude device were rejected, it was proclaimed sometime during the century following the experiment with the gold pennies[7] that

---

[1] August 16, 1257.   [2] RUDING, *op. cit.*, Vol. I, p. 358.

[3] LIVERPOOL, *op. cit.*, p. 46.   [4] November 16.

[5] These pennies seem never to have gained popularity.—LIVERPOOL, *op. cit.*, p. 46.

[6] Edward I. coined groats, 4 pennies, but they did not become generally current until the reign of Edward III.—*Ibid.*, p. 31.

[7] Prior to 1336, when provisions were made for the coinage of half-pennies and farthings.—RUDING, *op. cit.*, Vol. I, pp. 402, 408.

whoever, whether in buying or selling, should refuse any half-penny or farthing of lawful metal and proper form, should be seized as a contemner of the king's majesty, be thrown into prison, and suffer the punishment of the pillory.

In 1343 a second effort was made to introduce gold into the coinage system. Edward III. then coined the noble[1] and ordered it to be current at a certain value. Finding that this valuation was incorrect, and that the coins were overvalued, it was subsequently proclaimed[2] that no one should be forced to take them against his will. In the same year another set of coins was issued to be current at a different value, but it was ordered that they need not be taken in payments of less than twenty shillings.[3] Soon afterward, possibly because they had become popular, possibly to accustom the people to their use, it was ordered that these coins should not be refused in any payment whatever.[4]

From these illustrations, taken from the earlier portion of the period, it may be concluded that in cash transactions the money of gold and silver which was issued from the king's mint as lawful money, or to be current throughout the realm, was good in all cash payments, unless limitations or exceptions were expressly made known ; that is to say, of different forms of money current at any time the buyer had the right to select the form to be used. Coming to a more recent date, the same fact may be established. In 1662, for example, a certain base money had been issued for use in Ireland, and was ordered to be current in England also, except that no one should be compelled to take more than two in every twenty shillings of the baser kind.[5]

[1] See p. 33. These coins were issued January 27, 1343. The noble, $\frac{1}{70}$ of a pound of gold, $23\frac{1}{2}$ fine, was declared current at 6s., a ratio of 12$\frac{13724}{6235}$ to 1.—LIVERPOOL, *op. cit.*, p. 49.

[2] July 9, 1344.—KENYON, *Gold Coins of England*, p. 16.   [3] *Ibid.*, p. 18.

[4] See below, p. 33; HALE, *op. cit.*, Vol. I, p. 193.

[5] RUDING, *op. cit.*, Vol. II, p. 333. Similarly, when the minor copper coinage was introduced (1672), the limitation upon its currency was expressed.—*Ibid.*, p. 344.

An apparent exception to this rule is found by Lord Liverpool[1] in the fact that in 1663 the mint indenture providing for the issue of guineas declared that twenty shillings should be the legal value of the coin, while the authorities made no effort to enforce this rate when the coin became generally current at from twenty-one to twenty-two shillings. Color is lent to this view by the fact that the attorney-general was directed by an order in council to issue a proclamation declaring the coins current at the rate of the mint indenture, and no such proclamation was ever issued; while in 1717, when the guinea was declared to be a twenty-one shilling piece, such a proclamation issued, and every indication was given of intention to enforce it.[2] But the case of Dixson v. Willows,[3] already cited, shows this to be no more than a seeming exception, if an exception at all.

The method of enforcing the provisions here discussed becomes of interest. It was the method of imposing a penalty of greater or less severity for their violation; that is to say, the police power of the state was invoked in their support.

The question arises as to whether or not the Crown was bound by the rates indicated in the proclamation and indentures, and whether they applied to all royal revenues. It may be said at least that in those instruments no exception[4] is made with regard to the royal revenues; and yet there are acts of the Crown, or petitions in Parliament, which indicate that in these matters as in others the poor and lowly in position were imposed upon, not only by the king's officers, but by the great lords or their receivers. For

---

[1] *Op. cit.*, p. 76.   [2] *Ibid.*, p. 95.

[3] Or Dixson v. Willoughs, 3 SALKELD (English Reports), 238.

[4] An interesting exception to this fact may be cited: In 1689, when James II. was becoming desperate, he issued in Ireland "brass money" (six-penny pieces of brass and copper), declaring by his proclamation that they should be current in all payments, except the duties of customs and excise on importation of foreign goods, money left in trust, etc.—RUDING, *op. cit.*, Vol. II, p. 363.

example, in 1343 the Commons petitioned that the sheriffs and other officers of the king should receive for debts due him half-pennies as well as sterlings, and that all the great men and others of the realm should receive half-pennies for the debts, rents, and services due them, and that the half-penny should be of the same weight as the sterling (proportionately) and of as good silver, or be wholly put down;[1] but they received only an evasive answer to their prayer.[2] And in 1504 it was declared by proclamation that, "pence being silver and having the king's print, should be current to him in all his receipts and to all his receivers, and to all other lords, spiritual and temporal, and their receivers, and to all others within the realm."[3]

And from a proclamation issued by Henry VIII. at the time of his first debasement of the coinage (1526), wherein the dates at which the new values are to apply to antecedent obligations are carefully fixed,[4] it may be inferred that, making allowances for the influences referred to,[5] the same values prevailed in payments to the king's officers as in those to other individuals.

The commercial and industrial development of the sixteenth and seventeenth centuries, necessitating, as it did, freedom from governmental interference,[6] and transferring the emphasis to time transactions, as commercial life grew more complex and industrial processes involved more and more the time element, renders the class of cash transactions and regulations regarding the money to be used in

[1] *Ibid.*, Vol. I, p. 417.

[2] Indeed, a similar petition was offered three years later (1346), and seems to have been granted.—*Ibid.*, p. 431.

[3] See *Ibid.*, Vol. II, p. 59, for a similar provision.   [4] *Ibid.*, Vol. II, p. 78.

[5] See Statutes 7 and 8 William III., chap. 1; 8 William III., chap. 2; 8 and 9 William III., chap. 6—cited by LIVERPOOL, *op. cit.*, p. 83, for evidence of express permission to receive the clipped and defective coin prior to and during the great recoinage.

[6] It was in 1531 that Gresham protested against the restrictions on exchanges of different forms of money as injurious to Engligh trade.—RUDING, *op. cit.*,Vol. II, p. 82.

them interesting chiefly from the historical and theoretical point of view. Interest now centers in transactions involving time, and, as was said before,[1] the more general use of the words "legal tender" is in connection with this limited class of operations.

Turning, then, to time transactions, to executory contracts, of them, too, it may be said that in the English law all "lawful money," all money issued from the mints as current money, was a legal tender in satisfaction of debts,[2] unless the contrary was expressed or limitations were imposed.

It was the doctrine of the middle ages that for every commodity or service there was a just money equivalent.[3] This had been the dictum of the Roman law. "However diversified may be the object of an obligation, it is always transferable, in the eyes of the law, into the payment of a certain sum of money."[4] Though the English law of contract was not fully developed before the time of Henry VIII., the action of debt which lay to recover a sum of money was one of the early actions developed, being in use at least as early as the time of Henry I., and it is from the pleas allowed in defense of such action that we have the word "tender." The debtor could of course discharge his obligation by payment of the sum claimed; but sometimes, when there was dissatisfaction on the part of the creditor, he could acquit himself by tender to the creditor of the amount admitted by him as due. Should the creditor refuse the sum tendered, the debtor could then deposit it with the court, leaving with the court the question of the adequacy of the tender.

---

[1] Chap. I, p. 2.

[2] "A debt is an obligation arising out of contract express or implied, as of a lending, or borrowing, or letting out, or some other just cause inducing a contract." —GLANVIL (Beames's Translation), book X, chap. 3.

[3] ASHLEY, *op. cit.*, p. 163.

[4] POSTE, *Institutes of Gaius* (ed. 3), pp. 340, 341.

The doctrine of the law as finally developed was that for every wrong involved in breach of contract there was, as in case of goods and services, a money equivalent, a money compensation. Only in so far as, by the payment of money damage, the parties could be put into the position in which they would have been had there been no breach, did the common law attempt to give relief.[1]

In deciding the question whether, when an alteration had been made in the money of the realm, a contract made before the alteration should be satisfied in the coin current at the time of making the agreement or in that current at the maturity of the obligation, the courts might have adopted either of two possible theories:

On the one hand, it might have been said that the logic of the doctrine that there was always a money equivalent for any breach of contract involved the requirement that in actions for the payment of money such money should be required of the debtor as was a fair equivalent for what he had agreed to pay. This would not have involved the decision that there could have been no alteration in the relative value of money to commodities, which would have been obviously impossible; but it would have necessitated the decision that such changes as had resulted from an arbitrary exercise of power should not apply to pre-existing obligations.

On the other hand, it might be held that the supreme authority which lends its force to bring about the satisfaction of the obligation may determine wholly the conditions on which that force will be exerted; that is, the state may say to the creditor that his claim will be enforced if he will submit to conditions imposed. Such a conclusion is to a certain extent inevitable. Conditions of time, of

[1] Herein lay one of the deficiencies of the common law, leading to the development of the court of chancery, which gave remedy, not by money damage, but by requiring specific performance of the agreement.

place, of form, etc., must be prescribed in order to insure the final settlement of controversies, to prevent the debtor from being harassed, etc. But when the state prescribes conditions which require of the creditor that he sacrifice what is morally and justly due him in order to obtain the advantage of the administration of justice, those conditions partake of the nature of a selling of justice. And against this the Crown was pledged by the provision in Magna Charta, " to none will we sell, deny, or defer justice." [1]

This position, however, was practically that taken by the courts. The Crown was the fountain and source of justice, and could prescribe the terms on which that justice would be administered. This doctrine was based fully and frankly on the theory of the royal prerogative. Owing, perhaps, to the amount of governmental regulation and the lack of general freedom of intercourse, there seems to be no question as to the royal power in this respect prior to the reign of Edward VI. In 1552–53, at the Hilary term of the year 6 and 7 Edward VI., we have the case of Poug v. DeLindsay [2], as follows: " In debt on bond in payment of £24 sterling, plea of tender that at the time of payment of said sum of money certain money was current in England in the place of sterlings, called Pollards, held, that if at the time appointed for payment a base money is current in lieu of sterling, tender at the time and place of that base money is good and the creditor can recover no other."

And in 1601, the forty-third year of Elizabeth's reign, the same question came up in the great legal-tender case known as Brett's Case, the " Case of *Mixt Monies:* "

"*April, 43 Eliz. Brett* bought wares of one *Gilbert* a merchant in London, and became bound to him in £200

---

[1] "*Nulli vendemus, nulli negabimus, nulli differemus rectum aut justitiam.*"— *Magna Charta*, chap. 40; STUBBS, *Select Charters, etc.*, p. 301.

[2] DYER (English Reports), 82A. This case is cited in the dissenting opinion in Griswold v. Hepburn, 2 DUVAL (Ky.), 71.

conditioned for the payment of one hundred pound *Sterling* current and lawful money of *England* in *September* following at *Dublin* in *Ireland:* 24th May, *43 Eliz.* the queen sent to *Ireland* certain mixt money from the tower of *London* with the usual stamp and inscription, and declared by her proclamation, that it should be lawful and current money of *Ireland, viz.* a shilling for a shilling, and sixpence for sixpence, and that accordingly it should pass in payment, and none to refuse, and declared that from the 10th of *July* next all other money should be decried and esteemed only as bullion and not current money. Upon the day of payment *Brett* tendered the £100 in this mixt money, and resolved on great consideration that the tender was good, the place of payment being in *Ireland* and the day of payment happening after the proclamation was made; that altho this were not in truth *Sterling*, but of a baser allay, nor a money current in *England* by the proclamation, yet the payment being to be made in *Ireland*, it was, as to that purpose, current money of *England;* but if the day had been passed before the proclamation, then he must have answered the value as it was when payment was to have been made."

The report of this case is given in full as quoted from Sir John Davis by Sir Matthew Hale, because it is the basis of the English law of tender.[1] Thus the question was squarely raised whether the money with which a contract should be fulfilled was that current at the time of making the agreement or that current at the time of payment, and the law was settled in favor of the latter.

It has been said previously that the law regulating cash transactions was sanctioned by penal provisions. In the case of time transactions, such provisions are evidently unneces-

---

[1] Another case seems to have been decided in the same way in the same year, but of the decision only a quotation has been available. The substance of that is that every coin legitimated by royal proclamation becomes legal tender.— Wade's Case, cited from 43 Eliz. 406 by Rot.; HALE, *op. cit.*, Vol. I, p. 192.

sary. The power of the courts to declare a contract satisfied and the debtor acquitted of all obligation, *i. e.*, the civil power of the courts, is obviously adequate. In this power the law found its sanction.

In cash transactions, then, the buyer had the right of selecting the form of money to be used. In the same way, in time transactions the debtor had the power of choice as to the form of money in which his obligation would be satisfied.

The significance of this state of the law was that every act of state dealing with the lawful money of the realm, altering it in any way, was a legal-tender act, affecting the value of the monetary unit to be employed by any subject in the payment of his debts.

CHAPTER V

EXERCISE OF THE COINAGE POWER BY THE ENGLISH GOVERNMENT

Original Standard of Coinage — Attempt through Debasement to Obtain Good Circulating Medium — Efforts to Secure International Currency — Reasons for Later Debasement — Chaotic Condition under Henry VIII. — Efforts to Obtain Concurrent Circulation of Gold and Silver Coin.

IF the conclusions of the preceding chapters are accepted, there may be obtained from a survey of the acts of the Crown issuing new coin, altering coin already in circulation, or legitimating foreign coin, a view of the legal-tender policy of the English government. The presentation of such a view will be attempted in the present chapter.

For convenience, the long period to be discussed may be divided and those reigns considered together concerning which it is possible to make general statements. These divisions include, first, the reign of Henry II., Richard I., John, Henry III., covering the years from 1154 to 1272; second, the reigns of Edward I. and Edward II. (1272–1326/7); third, that of Edward III. (1326/7); fourth, from the accession of Richard II. through the reign of Henry VII.; fifth, the reigns of Henry VIII., Edward VI., Mary, and Elizabeth (1377–1602/3); sixth, and last, from the reign of James I. through that of George IV. (1602/3–1816).

Before proceeding to this discussion, it should first be remarked of the original standard of coinage in England that at the time of the Conquest the standard unit at the English mint was the *tower*, or *Saxon*, pound of silver, weighing 5,400 grains, and $\frac{37}{40}$ fine; that is, 11 oz. 2 dwt. of silver to

18 dwts. alloy. This remained the unit until 1527, when Henry VIII. substituted the Troy pound of 5,760 grains.[1] To the tower pound the pound in tale conformed, being divided into twenty shillings, which were in turn divided into twelve pence, or esterlings.[2]

As in many other respects, so in the coinage, the Conqueror left affairs as he found them, and retained the weight, standard, and denomination of his predecessors. At first only pennies (sterlings) were coined; then fractions of a penny; and finally, in the time of Henry VII. (1485–1509), silver coins of higher denominations. Up to this time these denominations denoted only money of account; and payments of large sums were doubtless often made by weight[3]—a practice which diminished the inconvenience arising from having coins of only one denomination and that a low one.

It has been noted[4] that one of the reforms promised by Henry II. when he came to the throne (1154) was the reformation of the coinage. This was carried out by him, and there seems to be some evidence that he raised somewhat the standard of fineness.[5] At all events, from the date of his accession until 1299[6] no alteration for the worse took place.

During this period there were, however, interesting occasions for the exercise of the coinage power, growing out of the worn state of the English coins and the importation of poorer money from the continent. As the uncertainties con-

---

[1] This tower pound was probably identical with the unit of Charles the Great. —See KENYON, *Gold Coins of England*, p. 84; RIDGEWAY, *Origin of Metallic Currency and Weight Standards*, p. 385; CUNNINGHAM, *Growth of English Industry and Commerce in Mediæval Times*, p. 118.

[2] The same word "sterling" or "esterling" or "aesterling," designated the standard fineness of the silver metal, $\frac{37}{40}$ fine, and the coin, the penny, made of that standard. Note Blackstone's use of it in passages cited, p. 12. "As in the esterling" meant "as in the penny of the good old times." On the continent it was a general term for the money of England.—RUDING, *op. cit.*, Vol. I, p. 17; compare HALE, *op. cit.*, Vol. I, p. 189.

[3] MADOX, *History of the Exchequer*, Vol. I, p. 272.

[4] P. 9.   [5] HALE, *op. cit.*, Vol. I, p. 190.   [6] 28 Edw. I.

nected with the value of the coin, which constituted the only circulating medium, caused great distress among the people, a general council "of all the nobles of England, bishops, earls, and barons," was held before the king at Oxford, in the year 1247. It was then proposed to look for the remedy in an alteration of the standard.[1] This proposition was rejected; but during the next year (1248) resort was had to a great recoinage, under the following conditions:[2] First, from every pound was taken thirteen pence to cover cost of coinage;[3] offices of exchange were established at which the new money could be obtained for the old, but they were few and distant the one from the other, so that persons had to suffer loss of time and strength in making the journey; and the new money was given for the old only by weight, which of course meant a greatly diminished number of pieces. These were surely arduous terms. Matthew Paris, the historian of this early period,[4] says that where thirty shillings should have been received scarce twenty were got. So great were the obstacles that it was found necessary to "cry down"[5] the old coins, which seems to have been rarely done in English history;[6] but the purpose seems to have been an honest purpose.

Again, the effort to obtain a good circulating medium may be seen in the attempt of the king to introduce gold coins into England, to which allusion has been made.[7] The attempt failed, perhaps from simple conservatism on the part of the people, perhaps because the method employed was a poor one;[8]

[1] RUDING, op. cit., Vol. I, p. 353.

[2] 32 Henry III.—Ibid., p. 355.

[3] This included a seigniorage of 7d. in the pound.

[4] Cited, ibid., p. 370.

[5] Deprive of its currency or legal-tender quality.

[6] Ibid., p. 355.   [7] P. 18.

[8] These coins were known as "pennies" and were 199/200 fine. They weighed as much as two silver pennies, or 45 grains, and were to pass at twenty pennies.—LIVERPOOL, op. cit., p. 45.

but ruler and people were alike honestly seeking remedies for the distressing condition of the money of the realm.

In the year 1299 Edward I. caused the first reduction in the legal weight of the penny to be made. He then had the pound weight divided into 20s. 3d.,[1] and thus reduced the penny by $1\frac{19}{81}$ per cent. There seems to have been no other reason for this than the desire to adapt the legal value of the coin to the worn condition of those already in use.[2] The king was but adopting the suggestion made by the council of nobles a half century before.[3]

During the reign of Edward I. (1272–1307) and his successor,[4] efforts were chiefly directed toward preventing the importation of "weak" foreign money, of which there was an increasing quantity as intercourse with the continent became freer. Thus, in 1292, there was enacted under the authority of Parliament the *statutum de moneta*, consisting of three parts. The first of these seems to be a true statute, or act of general legislation, and provided that no one should presume to pay or receive any money but the coins of the king of England, of Ireland, and of Scotland, on pain of forfeiture;[5] nor should anyone bring into England money except for his expenses, or, unless driven by tempest, land at any port other than those at which there were inspectors, to whom the amounts and kinds of money brought in should be made known.[6]

Edward II. made no change in his coins; but he found them in a sadly depreciated[7] condition, because of such practices as clipping, or bringing in light foreign coin; and so in 1310 it was ordered by proclamation that money should

---

[1] *Ibid.*, p. 39. [2] RUDING, *op. cit.*, Vol. I, p. 388.

[3] 1247. [4] Edward II., 1307–1326/7.

[5] 20 Edward I., chap. 4, cited by RUDING, *op. cit.*, Vol. I, p. 382.

[6] The other portions of the statute simply looked to the enforcement of these provisions.

[7] It seems to have been depreciated by one-half.—*Ibid.*, p. 399.

be current at the value it had borne in the reign of Edward
I., and that no one should on that account enhance the price
of his goods, "because it was the King's pleasure that the
coins should be kept up to the same value as they were wont
to bear." [1]

Passing to the next period, the long reign of Edward III.
(1326/7–77), it may be said, in general, that he was facing
the same difficulties connected with a worn, depreciated, and
confused money which had baffled his predecessors and were
then confronting his contemporaries on the continent. [2]

The inadequacy of the amount of bullion brought to the
mints he tried to overcome by requiring the exporters of wool
to pledge the importation of a certain amount of bullion for
every sack of wool exported. [3] The difficulties arising from the
importation of inferior foreign coin he met by the attempt to
agree with the Flemish upon certain principles to be applied
in the coinage, with the understanding that the coins of each
country should be given currency in the other. [4] He also provided for the coinage of half pence and farthings, [5] and introduced the coinage of gold into his monetary system. [6] But
he seems finally to have become discouraged, and resorted to
the debasement of the silver coins and of his new gold pieces.

The difficulties of the situation and the method of coping
with them may be illustrated by the incidents of the Turney,
a certain "black money" made in Ireland and circulated in

[1] *Ibid.*, p. 399.

[2] CUNNINGHAM, *op. cit.*, p. 354, n. The general principles of coinage and
monetary problems were arousing attention at the time, as is evidenced by the
appearance of the first treatise on money—that of Oresme, Bishop of Lisieux, *De
Mutatione Monetarum.*

[3] 40s. was the sum proposed in 1339; 13s. 4d. was decreed in 1340.—RUDING, *op. cit.*,
Vol. I, p. 410.

[4] *Ibid.*, p. 416. The Flemish coins, while allowed to circulate, were not to be
forced into circulation, but taken by those " who of their own accord would receive
them."—*Ibid.*, pp. 416, 421.

[5] *Ibid.*, p. 408.

[6] KENYON, *op. cit.*, p. 17. This was a part of the plan for an international
currency.

England, "to the injury of the king's sterling money and his no little loss and prejudice." Proclamation was therefore made to prohibit the circulation of it on pain of forfeiture of money and goods.[1] But great inconvenience was found to result from the prohibition, on account of the scarcity of sterling money. When this was made known to the king it was provided that if, on inquiry, it should be found more advantageous to the public to allow the circulation of the black money, a proclamation should issue authorizing it until an adequate supply of other money was provided.[2]

Four years later (1343) another unsuccessful attempt was made to introduce gold into the English coinage system. After an examination before Parliament of merchants, goldsmiths, and moneyers, experts in the subject, it was ordered that one kind of gold money should be made both in England and in Flanders,[3] to be current at such weight, alloy, and value as the king and Council should appoint, all other gold money being prohibited in both countries. Accordingly, three kinds of gold coin were provided for by an indenture: The florin, weighing 108 grains, the half and the quarter florin, of proportionate weight, and of a fineness equal to 23 carats, $3\frac{1}{2}$ grains of pure gold to $\frac{1}{2}$ grain of alloy.[4] These coins were at first declared current at 6s. 3d. and 1s. 6d., respectively;[5] but the following year (1344) it was found that they were rated too high in terms of silver,[6] and it was accordingly ordered that they should be taken in payment only with the consent of those to whom they were offered; and then a month later they were declared to be bullion to be received according to their value as such.[7] Another experiment yet had

---

[1] An illustration of the mode of sanction in legal-tender provisions applying to executed contracts.

[2] RUDING, *op. cit.*, Vol. I, p. 409.   [3] KENYON, *op. cit.*, pp. 17, 18.

[4] $\frac{191}{192}$ fine.

[5] January 27, 1343 —Cobbett's *Parliamentary History*, Vol. I, p. 200.

[6] See p. 35, n. 4.   [7] RUDING, *op. cit.*, Vol. I, p. 421.

evidently to be tried. The next gold coins attempted were called "nobles," and weighed $138\frac{6}{13}$ grains[1] of gold of the same fineness. They were declared current at 6s. 8d. Their coinage took place during the year in which the florins were called in,[2] and they were not to be forced in payment of sums less than twenty shillings.[3] This experiment succeeded and gold became a permanent element in the coinage system of England.

In this same year (1344) occurred the second debasement of the silver coinage,[4] and two years later (1346) both the silver and the gold coins were reduced in weight.[5] By this change the silver pound in tale[6] was reduced to a weight less by more than 10 per cent. than its original weight, while the gold pound weight was divided into 42, instead of $37\frac{1}{2}$, nobles, and the gold coin thus reduced by more than 7 per cent. to pass current at 6s. 8d. as before.[7]

Notwithstanding the reduction here noted, in 1351[8] the English coins are said to have been " so much better than the coins of any other nation that they were exported and base money brought into the realm, to the impoverishment of the people." Accordingly, both gold and silver coins were reduced in weight; the gold noble to 120 grains,[9] and the silver shilling to 216.[10]

[1] That is, the pound was divided into 39½ such coins.

[2] 1344.

[3] A case of limited legal tender, the limit being a minimum. It might be stated that the ratio of these to silver was 11 $\frac{1775}{2409}$: 1, while that of the previously coined florins had been 12 $\frac{1288}{2409}$: 1.—LIVERPOOL, op. cit., pp. 40, 50.

[4] Ibid., p. 39. The pound was divided into 22s. 2d., thus debasing the pound in tale 8 + per cent.

[5] Ibid.; KENYON, op. cit., p. 21.

[6] The pound in weight was then divided into 22s. 6d.

[7] This made the ratio 11 $\frac{637}{1033}$: 1.—LIVERPOOL, op. cit., p. 51.

[8] This date is given by RUDING, op. cit., Vol. I, p. 436.—LIVERPOOL gives 1353, op cit., p. 51.

[9] From 128½ to pass as before at 8s. 6d.

[10] From 240 grains. This made the ratio 11 $\frac{158}{433}$: 1.—KENYON, op. cit., p. 21; LIVERPOOL, op. cit., pp. 40, 51.

As no other alteration was made in the coinage during this reign, or indeed for half a century, it may be well to inquire into the motives leading to these three alterations in the coinage and their effects on the condition of affairs then existing in the kingdom. In the first place, they caused great dissatisfaction among the people. The bishop of Winchester, who seems to have been held responsible for the second of the three debasements, became most unpopular, and it was said of him that " he loved the King's commoditie better than the wealth of the realme and common people." [1] It is to be noted also that the statute to which reference has been made,[2] attempting to limit the royal power, dated from the year of the third alteration; from which it may be inferred that this method was not satisfactory to the people.

The question suggests itself whether the profits which arose from calling in and recoining the money of the realm did not furnish an adequate explanation of these debasements. This question indicates the necessity of at least a brief discussion of the nature of those profits and the part they seem to have played in controlling royal policy.

The profit arising from the operations of the mint assumed two forms : that arising from the *shere*,[3] or remedy allowed because of the rudeness of the art of coinage, and that known as *seigniorage*, or contribution to the king, over and above the cost of mintage,[4] claimed by virtue of the prerogative.[5] Of the shere it is needless to speak here, as advantage seems to have been taken of it very rarely,[6] but seigniorage was an avowed right claimed by the sovereigns of Europe. It seems to have been of Gothic rather than of Roman origin, and was an important element in the royal revenues. There

---

[1] See LIVERPOOL, *op. cit.*, p. 39, n.   [2] See above, p. 11.

[3] RUDING, *op. cit.*, Vol. I, p. 185.   [4] "Brassage."   [5] LIVERPOOL, *op. cit.*, p. 116.

[6] Elizabeth is charged with having underpaid the master of the mint, with the understanding that he might recoup himself by making the coins as light as possible within the limits.—See RUDING, *op. cit.*, Vol. I, p. 185.

were two methods of appropriating this forced contribution. The method which prevailed on the continent in the earlier times was that of taking the profit out of the coin itself, returning to the merchant who had brought bullion or coins to the mint a given number reduced in weight.[1] The practice which prevailed in England, however, was this: The bullion was first assayed and coined, the seigniorage and brassage then deducted in the coins already made, and the remaining coins returned to the merchant who had brought the bullion to the mint.[2] The amounts to be deducted were prescribed in the indenture with the master of the mint. For example, in the first coinage of gold nobles (1344), according to the indenture, from a pound of gold £15 sterling were to be made. Of these, 3s. 6d. was to cover expenses of mintage, £1 was to be deducted for the king, and the remainder, £13 16s. 6d., was then to be given to the merchant.[3] The following year (1345) the sum to be held by the master of the mint was reduced to 2s. in the pound,[3] that for the king to 5s., which would indicate that gold was not being brought in adequate quantities to the mint, and greater inducements in the form of diminished cost were offered.

At the same time, for the coinage of silver the seigniorage was 6d. for every pound weight, and the allowance to the master of the mint 8d., leaving for the merchant 21s. for every tower pound of silver brought to the mint.[4]

[1] LIVERPOOL, op. cit., p. 118.

[2] RUDING, op. cit., Vol. I, p. 184. Sometimes the larger part of the king's share was granted to induce merchants to bring bullion.—See ibid., p. 434.

[3] Ibid., p. 419 (see note b).

[4] Ibid., p. 427. It would seem that there should be some definite relation between the legal ratio of gold to silver coin and the ratio actually existing under the regulations of the mint. For example, if a merchant took gold and silver bullion to the mint to be coined, he should have got a number of coins of each metal which would bear to each other a ratio approximating the legal ratio. Such was not the case, however. In 1344-45 the legal ratio of gold to silver was $1 : 12\frac{43744}{44444}$, while the ratio obtained by comparing the value in coin of a pound of gold with that of the same weight of silver to the merchant who took the bullion to the mint was

Of course, when a debasement occurred the holder of coins of the earlier weight would gladly bring them to the mint, as he would obtain a greater number of coins of the diminished weight, and so a profit on them, unless they were greatly worn and clipped; and, making allowance for these factors, the king would have his seigniorage on all the money of the realm.

Doubtless Edward III. felt the need of increasing his revenues in all possible ways;[1] but there does not seem evidence to convict him of corrupt motives in dealing with his coinage. The state of the English money was deplorable, because of the exportation of full-weight English money[2] and the importation of lighter foreign pieces, especially Scotch;[3] so that the alterations seem rather attempts to increase the amount in circulation, to prevent exportation, and to adapt the legal to the actual value of the coins in circulation.[4]

With Edward's successor, Richard II. (1377–99), was inaugurated the policy which ripened into the mercantile policy, and from the time of his reign a good currency as a public service and the accumulation of treasure as a political necessity were sought.[5] The long period during which this

1:13½. A comparison of RUDING's Tables of the Seigniorage and of those giving the legal ratios between coins shows such differences to have been the rule, and not the exception.

[1] Because of the wars with France and the poverty of the people after the scourge of the black death (1348) and the growing power of Parliament.—GREEN, op. cit., pp. 429–61.

[2] See RUDING, op. cit., Vol. I, pp. 414, 438, 440, 445, 447, for petitions and provisions against carrying good money out of the realm.

[3] In 1355 the coins of Scotland of an earlier date, being of the English weight and standard, were allowed currency; it was found necessary in 1367 to prohibit the currency of any foreign money.—Ibid., pp. 443, 449. It should be noted that the function of exchanging coins of different metals or of different nationalities, with its attendant profits, was also monopolized by the government; see Ibid., pp. 422, 443. And this, as in the case of the coinage, was enforced by penal provisions.

[4] This is put in stronger terms by CARLILE, The Evolution of Modern Money, p. 101, when he says that never before the time of Henry VII. were alterations made for purposes of profit. See, also, ASHLEY, op. cit., p. 168.

[5] CUNNINGHAM, History of English Industry and Commerce in Mediæval Times, p. 377.

policy prevailed was interrupted by the chaotic condition prevailing during the reign of Henry VIII. (1509–1546/7) and his immediate successors. On that account the period may be subdivided, the years from the accession of Richard II. to the death of Henry VII. (1377–1509) being first considered together.

No alteration in the coinage occurred during the reign of Richard II., but in 1381 an interesting inquiry was conducted into the causes for its deplorable state, and various remedies were suggested.[1] A number of persons who might be considered experts were questioned before Parliament, and gave their views in brief replies to definite questions. As the state of the gold coinage demanded particular attention, it was suggested that gold should be allowed to pass by weight; and it was also proposed, if a recoinage should be determined upon, that the king should remit his seigniorage.[2] The only result of the inquiry seems to have been a statute prohibiting the exportation of the precious metals in any form,[3] and the provision for more rigorous police measures in support of this.[4] The petitions and complaints of the Commons with reference to the exportation of good and importation of bad money continued during this and the following reigns.[5]

The next alteration to be noticed occurred in 1411, when Parliament, "because of the great scarcity of money at this time within the realm of England, and because of other mischiefs and causes manifest," ordained[6] that the pound of gold should be divided into 50 nobles[7] and the pound of silver into 30 shillings.[8]

---

[1] RUDING, op. cit., Vol. I, p. 463, seq.   [2] This was 3s. 6d. in the pound.

[3] Except for certain purposes to France.   [4] Ibid., p. 468.

[5] Ibid., pp. 458, 461, 462, 476, 483, 497, 502, 508.

[6] This act was called an ordinance, but had all the characteristics of a statute. —Ibid., p. 494.

[7] Instead of 45. That is, the new coin weighed 108 grains.

[8] Instead of 25. That is, the new shilling weighed 180 grains. As the nobles were to pass at the same nominal value, the ratio was $10\frac{479}{793}:1$.—LIVERPOOL, op cit., p. 52.

The coin seems at this time to have been the subject of corrupt practice on all sides. Individuals clipped, counterfeited, and exported it; and it appears from the account given by the historian Daniel[1] that corrupt methods prevailed at the mint. In fact, the gold coin suffered so that in 1421 it was found necessary to ordain its passage by weight.[2] The account of this particular debasement should not be left without noting the fact that it occurred in accordance with an act of Parliament.

An interesting ordinance in the nature of a legal-tender provision was published in 1429.[3] Foreign merchants had introduced a custom of refusing to exchange their goods for silver and accepting only gold coins, which they carried out of the realm. The king, therefore, ordained that no alien merchant should " constrain or bind any of his liege people by promise, covenant, or liege to make true payment in gold for any manner of debt due to him, nor refuse to receive payment in silver," upon penalty of the double value of the sum due.[4]

In 1445, an ordinance providing for something very like the token coins of today was published. Because of the lack of small coins, the Commons petitioned that the pound of silver might be divided into thirty-three instead of thirty shillings, to be coined into half-pennies and farthings, which should be given currency to this extent — that in every payment of twenty shillings twelve pence might be of these lighter coins.[5] The ordinance was to endure for two years, at the discretion of the king.

In 1464, because of the scarcity of money and the small

---

[1] Quoted in COBBETT, *Parliamentary History*, Vol. I, p. 313.

[2] *Ibid.*, p. 340.   [3] 8 Henry VI., chap. 28.

[4] RUDING, *op. cit.*, Vol. II, p. 14. The legislation applied evidently to both time and cash transactions.

[5] *Ibid.*, p. 18. "There is no comment by which any inference as to the extent or effect of this ordinance can be obtained."

amount of bullion brought to the mints, another reduction
was made. The silver pound was then divided into 37s. 6d.[1]
The weight of the gold noble was not diminished, but its
nominal value was increased from 6s. 8d. to 8s. 4d., and a new
gold coin[2] was introduced.[3]   It may be noticed that by this
time the silver pound in tale had been reduced by $46\frac{2}{3}$ per
cent. of the weight it had prior to 1299.

At the end of Henry VII.'s reign the condition of the
money of the country was such that resort was had to the
use of private tokens to supply the lack in the circulating
medium.[4] The cupidity and miserliness of the king were
almost boundless, so that the administration of justice was
abused, vigorous prosecutions were carried on, and excessive fines imposed to fill his coffers.[5] Yet the abuse of his
coinage power for the sake of gain was not resorted to. That
remained for his spendthrift son.[6]

In presenting the history of the following period no detailed
account of the changes wrought in the money of the realm
will be attempted. It was a period of chaos. The policy of
Henry VIII., after he had dissipated the treasure left by
his father, was the policy of a spendthrift; and, like other
spendthrifts, he resorted to all possible measures to secure
means of indulgence. The forms of law were often preserved
when the spirit was grossly violated. This was particularly
true in his treatment of the coinage. The prerogative had
been confirmed without limit in the time of Henry VII., as

---

[1] That is, the shilling was reduced from 180 grains to 144.

[2] The "angel," current at 6s. 8d., the old value of the noble, but weighing 81 +
grains, instead of 108 grains; making the ratio of gold to silver 1:11$\frac{161}{625}$.—LIVER-
POOL, *op. cit.*, p. 53.

[3] RUDING, *op. cit.*, Vol. II, p. 33; LIVERPOOL, *op. cit.*, p. 40.

[4] These circulated as late as the beginning of the seventeenth century.—RUDING,
op. cit., p. 69.

[5] *Ibid.*, p. 64.

[6] It is possible that he closed his eyes to corrupt practices in his mint. That
would be different from an abuse of his prerogative.—See RUDING, *op. cit.*, Vol. II,
p. 60.

has been pointed out.[1] Of this he took advantage in every conceivable way.

The first alteration made by him, however, was not particularly alarming, and but carried out the policy which had led to former reductions—that of preventing exportation of English money for recoinage at foreign mints. This change was made in 1527, and by it the tower pound was divided into 42, instead of $37\frac{1}{2}$, shillings.[2]

The proclamation legitimizing these new coins is particularly interesting because of two features: It prohibited any increase of prices "under color of the money being enhanced,"[3] and by it the terms in which antecedent obligations were to be satisfied were carefully regulated.[4]

Never before had the standard of the metal of either gold or silver been altered. From the time at which Edward III. had successfully introduced gold into circulation,[5] $\frac{191}{192}$ had represented the proportion of fine metal to alloy in all gold coins. From the earliest coinage in England $\frac{37}{40}$ had represented the sterling silver. On both metals Henry laid sacrilegious hands. The fineness of the gold coins he reduced successively to $\frac{184}{192}$,[6] $\frac{180}{192}$,[7] $\frac{176}{192}$,[7] and $\frac{160}{192}$.[8]

The fineness of the silver coins he reduced to $\frac{10}{12}$, $\frac{6}{12}$, and $\frac{4}{12}$.[9] This debasement was carried one degree farther by Edward VI., when $\frac{3}{12}$ represented the proportion of precious metal to alloy in English silver coins.[10]

At this point may be given a brief account of the method

---

[1] See above, p. 13.

[2] The tower pound was divided in 42s. 2¼d., or the Troy pound already introduced into 45s. The shilling was now reduced from 144 to 131 grains. The nominal value of gold coins was changed, but no change in their weight or alloy occurred at this time.—LIVERPOOL, *op. cit.*, p. 41; RUDING, *op. cit.*, Vol. II, p. 74.

[3] That is, the nominal value increased, while the amount of metal remained the same; or, the nominal value left the same, while the amount of metal was diminished.

[4] *Ibid.*, pp. 78, 87.   [5] 1344.

[6] 1543.—KENYON, *op. cit.*, p. 94.   [7] 1544.—*Ibid.*, p. 95.

[8] 1545.—*Ibid.*, p. 95; see also p. 90.   [9] 1543.—LIVERPOOL, *op. cit.*, p. 98.

[10] RUDING, *op. cit.*, Vol. II, p. 108.

by which the coins were restored to a condition almost equal to their former weight and fineness. The gold coins had been debased to a smaller extent than the silver coins. The relative values set upon the coins [1] had been such as to over-value the silver in terms of gold, so that the gold coins were all hoarded. Edward VI. early gave his attention to the restoration of the coins, and the first effort put forth was in the direction of calling forth the hoarded gold. This was accomplished by raising the nominal value of the gold coins to a value one-third greater than that at which they had been estimated in 1527.[2] The next step was the issue of silver coins, likewise of one-third greater value.[3] The third step was to decry the base coins issued since 1527.[4] This was not done by one act, but two proclamations issued, by each of which they were reduced in legal value. They were finally wholly cried down by Elizabeth in 1660, after she had issued new coins of the original standard of fineness ($\frac{37}{40}$), and of the weight at which they had been made in 1527.[5] The act of crying down the coins seems to have been rarely performed in connection with English coins.[6] In those foreign jurisdictions within which frequent recoinages were had for purposes of profit[7] this process must have been a necessary one ; for only by some such compulsory act as this would the owners of coins have been induced to bring them to the mint to be recoined. Only by force could such a contribution to the king's revenues have been obtained.

---

[1] These values were (1545) 6$\frac{8}{11}$: 1 ; (1546) 5 : 1.—LIVERPOOL, *op. cit.*, p. 101.

[2] The sovereign which had been current for 22s. 6d. was made current for 30s. —RUDING, *op. cit.*, Vol. II, pp. 106 ff.

[3] The tower pound was divided into 56s. 3d.—LIVERPOOL, *op. cit.*, pp. 40, 108.

[4] April 30 and May 11, 1551. Resort was had to severe police measures to prevent an increase of prices.— RUDING, *op. cit.*, Vol. II, p. 118.

[5] LIVERPOOL, *op. cit.*, pp. 110, 111 ; RUDING, *op. cit.*, Vol. II, 137. This proclamation crying down the debased coins defends and explains the action of the queen in attempting to restore the coinage to something of its former excellence.

[6] See above, p. 29, n. 5.   [7] CARLILE, *op. cit.*, p. 101.

In the instances cited, however, may be observed an illustration of how the power to deprive coins of their legal-tender quality could be utilized for the sake of improving the condition of the money of the realm.

The restoration of the coins is counted one of the glories of Elizabeth's reign;[1] yet before the close of her career she allowed herself to make a final reduction. The silver tower pound was then divided into 58s. 1½d.,[2] and the gold coins were likewise reduced in weight.[3] The reasons which led to the debasements of this period are not difficult to find. Already, in 1513, the king, Henry VIII., had exhausted the millions left by his father and drained his subjects by repeated subsidies,[4] so that his chosen policy of foreign warfare was thwarted. It was not to be hoped that in the period during which "all the constitutional safeguards of English freedom were swept away," when arbitrary powers of taxation, legislation, and imprisonment were claimed and exercised,[5] such a resource as the coinage power would remain neglected. For the first debasement, in 1527, a reason was found in the difficulties of international trade;[6] for the later debasements under Henry no other reason need be sought than a desire to augment his revenues.[7]

The first debasement, under Edward VI., has a special interest, because it was frankly resorted to in order to gain a sum for the king's treasury with which the expenses of the

---

[1] FROUDE, *History of England from the Fall of Wolsey to the Death of Elizabeth* (N. Y., 1890), Vol. VII, p. 465.

[2] Instead of 56s. 3d.—LIVERPOOL, *op. cit.*, p. 41.

[3] So that the ratio was 11 ⁸⁹⁄₉₆ : 1 for coins of the old standard of fineness (¹¹⁄₁₂ fine), and 11¹⁄₁₀ : 1 for coins of the Crown standard (²²⁄₂₄ fine). The latter standard was that which prevailed, though coins of both standards circulated until 1732, when those of the ancient fineness were declared no longer current.—*Ibid.*, p. 32; KENYON, *op. cit.*, p. 100.

[4] GREEN, *Short History of the English People* (N. Y., 1880), p. 320.

[5] *Ibid.*, p. 341.   [6] See above, p. 40.

[7] COBBETT'S *Parliamentary History*, Vol. I, p. 559.

restoration of the coins might be undertaken. The king's journal bears witness to this.[1]

There remains to be considered the period from 1603, when Elizabeth died, until 1816, when silver was finally given a secondary position in the English system. During this period the weight and denominations of gold coins were altered in order to secure the concurrent circulation of coins of both metals; but no change was made by law in the character of the silver coins.[2]

At the time of the reduction in 1601 the legal ratio of gold to silver was lower than it had been at any time since the early part of the fifteenth century,[3] excepting, of course, the chaotic period under Henry VIII. From this time the value of gold bullion changed rapidly in terms of silver,[4] and although the mint ratios were frequently altered, all efforts to retain both metals in circulation failed. In 1604 the mint ratio of gold to silver was raised 10 per cent.—an increase not great enough, however, to bring gold from countries where it was more highly rated. In 1611–12 an alteration in the same direction, going too far, drove the silver out as the gold came in, causing so great a scarcity of silver that the old laws against exportation were revived and re-enacted.[5] No remedy was found until, by the simple passage of time,[6] in the development then in progress, the

---

[1] "April 10, 1551. Also it was appointed to make 20,000 pound weight for necessity somewhat baser to get gains 160,000 pounds clear, by which the debt of the realm might be paid, the country defended from any sudden attempt, and the coin amended."—Cited by RUDING, op. cit., Vol. II, p. 106; see also p. 108.

[2] The legislation in 1774, which will be noted, left them unaltered except as to their legal-tender power.—See below, p. 45.

[3] 1412.

[4] It was, in 1601, 10 $\frac{50}{80}\frac{11}{11}$: 1.—LIVERPOOL, op. cit., p. 58.

[5] See the proclamation cited by LIVERPOOL, op. cit., p. 69. Strangely enough another change in the same direction was made in 1620 (Ibid., p. 60), increasing the difficulty.—See RUSHWORTH, cited by LIVERPOOL, op. cit., p. 72.

[6] About the time of the beginning of the Commonwealth (1648).—Ibid., p. 78.

market value of gold in terms of silver overtook and soon passed the mint value of that metal.[1]

Added to the difficulties growing out of the maladjustment of the mint ratios there were still great inconveniences created by the fraudulent practices of counterfeiting and clipping. "So deplorable was the condition of the coin that nothing could be purchased without a dispute. On a fair or a market day the clamours, reproaches, the taunts, the curses, were incessant, and it was well if no booth was overturned, no head broken. . . . . The labourer found that the bit of metal which, when he received it, was called a shilling would barely, when he wanted to purchase a pot of beer, go as far as a sixpence."[2]

It was to meet these conditions that William, in 1695, threw upon Parliament the responsibility of finding a remedy. Resort was first had to new and more rigorous police measures. It was then proposed that the silver coins be again reduced in weight and the same remedy be applied that had been employed by Edward I.[3] four centuries before; that is, that the legal be adapted to the actual value of the coins: but this proposition was rejected, and the great recoinage of the silver of the realm was carried out in the years 1695–98, leaving the silver coins unchanged.[4] In 1662–63 there had been an alteration in the gold coins, caused by the market value of the gold in terms of silver creeping past the mint value. Those coins in circulation had been raised in value and new twenty shilling pieces had been issued, to be known as "guineas."[5] These coins had immediately become generally

---

[1] Rising probably little under 33 per cent. between 1604 and 1664.—*Ibid.*, p. 66.

[2] MACAULAY, *History of England*, Vol. V, p. 89.

[3] 1299.—See above, p. 30.

[4] See MACAULAY'S account, *op. cit.*, pp. 89 f.; LOCKE'S *Writings* (London, 1823), Vol. I, p. 131; LIVERPOOL, *op. cit.*, pp. 79 f.

[5] KENYON, *op. cit.*, p. 170. In 1670 these coins were reduced in weight, but left of the same nominal value and still circulated at a great advance on their mint value.— *Ibid.*, p. 170; LIVERPOOL, *op. cit.*, p. 62.

current at a value higher than the indenture rate, and in
1695 were passing generally at 30s.[1]

The provision for the recoinage of silver caused the gold
coins to fall in value relatively to silver, and it was resolved
by the House of Commons that they should not pass at a
value higher than 28s., which value was soon reduced to 26s.
On the basis of this resolution an act was passed imposing a
penalty on anyone who should receive or pay the twenty-
shilling piece or guinea at a higher rate than 26s.[2] This,
by another act of the same session, was reduced to 22s. In
1698 their price had fallen to 21s. 6d., at which rate they
were taken by the officers of the revenue. This rating of
the gold coin was not, however, such as to prevent the
exportation of silver, and in 1717[3] the legal value of the
guinea was reduced to 21s.[4]

Even this estimate of gold in terms of silver was still too
high, however, to bring silver into circulation,[5] and during
the century it remained scarce, so that gold became the
customary medium of exchange and the true standard of
payments.[6] In 1774 this state of facts was recognized by
legislation, and the legal-tender power of silver coin was
limited to £25 in any one payment, an excess of that
amount being paid by weight at the rate of 3s. 2d. to the
ounce.[7] This act, the duration of which was for two years,
was in 1776[8] renewed for another period of the same length.

[1] Kenyon, op. cit., p. 178.   [2] Ibid., p. 185.

[3] Liverpool, op. cit., pp. 94 f. Newton was then master of the mint, and it was
according to his suggestion that this step was taken.

[4] In his report Newton said that 8d. or 10d. would have to be taken from the value
of the guinea to make its value in England accord with that in other countries. He
proposed the subtraction of only 6d., however. In Horton, Silver Pound, Appendix,
this document may be found.—Cobbett, Parliamentary History, Vol. VII, pp. 523-5.

[5] Between 1717 and the end of the century the amount of silver coined at the
English mint was equal to £584,760 17s. 5½d.—Liverpool, op. cit., p. 96.

[6] As Carlile points out (op. cit., p. 742), silver coins were used in wage payments
and retail trade. They were, however, merely token coins, supported in value by
their relation to gold and by being actually, if not legally, limited in quantity.

[7] Ruding, op. cit., Vol. IV, p. 33.   [8] 16 George III., chap. 54.

In 1778[1] it was extended to 1783, when it was allowed to expire. In 1798[2] it was again revived, and continued until 1816, when the silver coins were reduced in weight and given the position of representative coins having a limited legal-tender power.[3] By this act gold was declared to be the standard coin of the realm; the silver pound was to be divided into shillings weighing $87\frac{3}{11}$ grains,[4] and it was decreed that silver coins should be considered representative coins, legal tender to the value of two guineas only.

RÉSUMÉ OF ENGLISH EXPERIENCE

The questions with which the inquiry began may now be called to mind, and such answers as have been obtained from the English experience stated.

In the first place, it appears that to the Crown belonged the power over the coinage. That power was exercised sometimes in such a manner as to accord with the expressed wishes of Parliament;[5] sometimes in such manner as deliberately to oppose those wishes;[6] sometimes without regard to whether Parliament had expressed any wish on the subject or not. It followed, therefore, that the money in which obligations were met could be altered by act of the Crown.

In the second place, the legal-tender quality was possessed by coins of both metals at specified relative values. There were inconsiderable limitations imposed upon one or the other, sometimes a maximum[7] and sometimes a

---

[1] 18 George III., chap. 45.

[2] 38 George III., chap. 59. These are cited by LIVERPOOL, *op. cit.*, p. 144.

[3] 56 George III., chap. 68. HORTON, *op. cit.*, p. 278, gives the report of the Lords of the Committee of Council on which the statute is based, as well as the proclamation following it.

[4] That is, the Troy pound was divided into 66s., the tower pound into 61⅞s., instead of 62s. and 58s. 1½d., as before. In 1817, the sovereign replaced the guinea as the 20s. piece of gold.—See *Ibid.*, p. 282; 57 George III., chap. 113.

[5] See above, pp. 32, 37.   [6] See above, p. 10.

[7] See above, p. 19.

minimum[1] limit being set; but, in general, it may be said that both gold and silver coins were a lawful tender; that in cash transactions the buyer, in time transactions the debtor, had the right to select the form of money to be employed. In the case of cash transactions it was found necessary to supplement this law by penal legislation and by legislation regulating prices.[2] But in the case of time transactions, the civil power of the courts was an adequate sanction.[3]

In the course of the period considered the pound in tale of silver was reduced by $65\frac{5}{9}\frac{5}{3}$ per cent. of its original weight.[4] The reasons which led to this result were two:[5] In the first place, there was the desire and purpose to remedy the " scarcity of coin," which was the chronic complaint of the people, the desire to secure a circulating medium, and to prevent criminal practices. The principles which should control the exercise of the power were ill understood. The idea of the coinage as the personal property of the prince, to be exploited for his benefit, was not wholly outgrown. Yet, on the whole, the review of the period is ill presented if it does not convey the impression of a general tendency on the part of government to do the right and honest thing and to meet the needs of the people in this vital matter of the money with which the ordinary transactions of life were performed.

In this fact—that mistaken policy controlled to so large an extent the exercise of the power—is found the answer to a question which must have suggested itself in the course of the discussion. That question is: Why did Parliament not succeed in its attempt to assume the coinage power as it succeeded in assuming the power over taxation? One reason for failure in this direction was the fact that Parliament had

[1] See above, p. 19.   [2] See above, p. 20.   [3] See above, p. 25.
[4] Before making silver a subsidiary element in the coinage.—LIVERPOOL, *op. cit.*, p. 42.
[5] *Ibid.*, p. 115.

no other remedy to propose, no other line of conduct to suggest than that pursued by the Crown. In 1247 it was the Council which proposed a debasement;[1] in 1411 Parliament effected one.[2] There seems to be no evidence to indicate that the power would have been more wisely exercised by Parliament than by the Crown.

But there was a second, and less worthy, motive which sometimes prevailed, namely, the desire for revenue. This was the controlling reason in the case of the debasements of Henry VIII. and Edward VI. No relief could have been expected from the degenerate Parliament of that time, however, willing as it was to give to kings' proclamations in general the force of law.[3]

It should be noted that the cases cited in which the law of tender was formulated by the courts [4] date from the period immediately subsequent to the abuses of Henry and from the period of parliamentary subservience. It should be likewise noted that from the period at which that law was formulated debasements cease. There is no intention of maintaining a direct connection between the formulation of the law and the cessation of abuses. The connection seems rather an indirect one. The law was acknowledged and acquiesced in. The Crown had the right to change the money in which contracts were settled, but the commercial development was such as to require a fixed standard of payments; the interests of the government and of the individual became closely identified through the organization of the public debt; the political development led to a keener sense of public morality; and, perhaps most important of all, the quickened intelligence and awakened public sentiment led to a more intelligent understanding of the principles which should govern the administration and exercise of such a power.

[1] See above, p. 29.　　　　　　　[2] See above, p. 37.
[3] See above, p. 8, n. 2.　　　　　[4] See above, p. 25.

CHAPTER VI

LEGAL TENDER IN THE COLONIES

Methods of Control over the Colonies — Idea that Legal-Tender Quality Must be Expressly Bestowed — Substitutes for Money Made a Legal Tender — Also Commodities at Specified Rates — Foreign Coin — Domestic Coin — Bills of Credit — Control Assumed by Parliament.

HAVING followed the story of the English policy with reference to legal-tender money to a date at which that policy seemed to culminate,[1] it is now proposed to turn back to an earlier date — that at which the colonies were established and new centers of activities acknowledging the sovereignty of the English government came into existence. The present chapter will deal with the subject of legal tender in the colonies which afterward became the United States of America.

As to the means by which the English government exercised control over the colonies, it may be said that in the earliest years of the colonial period[2] the superintendence of the king over the colonies was exercised by the Privy Council. In 1634 a board was created, called the "Lords Commissioners of Foreign Plantations," which consisted of certain high officers of state, empowered to make laws or ordinances affecting either the public condition or private property of the colonists.[3]

In 1643 the commission known as the "Lords of Trade and Plantations" was created, composed of a governor and a

---

[1] In the act of 1816.—See above, p. 46.

[2] Prior to 1634. Charters were granted to Virginia in 1606; to Plymouth in 1620; to the colony of Massachusetts Bay in 1628; etc.

[3] FROTHINGHAM, *Rise of the Republic of the United States* (6th ed.), p. 35.

49

council of whom five were peers and twelve members of the commons.[1]

In July, 1660, an order in Council was passed creating ten lords of the Council, or any three of them, a board to meet twice a week to receive petitions and papers relating to the colonies; and on November 7 of the same year the king created a commission[2] known as a "Council of Foreign Plantations," which was required to correspond with the governors of the colonies, and to devise means of bringing the colonies into a "more certain civil and uniform government." In 1674 this council was dissolved[3] and a committee of the Privy Council was appointed by the king to consider matters relating to the American colonies. This committee was to sit once a week and report to the Privy Council, and they continued to do so through the reign of James II.[4]

During this period[5] representative assemblies had been organized in the colonies, and these, together with the governor and council as co-ordinate branches, exercised the law-making power.[6] These assemblies were regarded as drawing their power from the Crown, and were limited in all their proceedings by the charters of the respective colonies, or by other confirmatory acts of the Crown.[7]

It is unnecessary here to speak of the revocation and regranting of the charters in the decade from 1680–90. This may be treated as a period of abnormal disturbance. During the reign of William and Mary, and during most of the period covered by the reigns of Anne and the first two Georges,[8] the colonial administration was arbitrary and showed strict adherence to the prerogative, though the

---

[1] FROTHINGHAM, *op. cit.*, p. 45.   [2] *Ibid.*, p. 50.

[3] Its powers had been increased in 1671.   [4] *Ibid.*, p. 77.

[5] Prior to the formation of representative assemblies the governor and council appointed by the Crown exercised these powers. — STORY, *Commentary on the Constitution of the United States* (3d ed.), § 43.

[6] FROTHINGHAM, *op. cit.*, p. 18.   [7] STORY, *op. cit.*, § 185.   [8] 1688–1760.

people through their assemblies shared in the control of local affairs. During this period the formal channel of communication between the Crown and the colonies was the "Lords of Trade and Plantations," created in 1696. This board, consisting at first of a president and seven members, was afterwards enlarged, and to it was assigned the general oversight of American affairs and the duty of recommending measures relating to the colonies.[1]

As to the power of Parliament to enact laws which should be binding on the colonies, there was much doubt. The home government always maintained the doctrine that Parliament could bind the colonies in all cases whatsoever, but no act was understood to apply to the colonies unless it was expressly declared to do so.

It was of course the policy of the colonists, so far as possible, to deny such authority, except when their necessities forced them to comply with parliamentary measures expressly extended to them ;[2] and some went so far as to deny that any act of Parliament could bind the colonies without their consent.[3]

The notions of rights and remedies which the colonists retained were those of British subjects as based on the common law. The power of the Crown over the coinage was admitted as part of the royal prerogative. The law of contracts, including that of debt and tender as found in the English law, was recognized by them.

[1] FROTHINGHAM, *op. cit.*, pp. 104, 107, 131.

[2] STORY, *op. cit.*, §§ 187, 188.

[3] FROTHINGHAM, *op. cit.*, p. 109, cites an interesting passage from an "Essay on Government" published in the colonies in 1701. "It is a great unhappiness that no one can tell what is law and what is not in the plantations. Some hold that the law of England is chiefly to be respected, and when that is defective the laws of the respective colonies are to take its place; others are of the opinion that the laws of the colonies are to take first place, and that the law of England is of force only when they are silent. Others there are who contend for the laws of the colonies in conjunction with those that were in force in England at the first settlement of the colony . . . . , alleging that we are not bound to observe any late acts of parliament except such only where the reason of the law is the same as in England."

While they had brought over to the new country little money, they retained their English method of accounting,[1] and "pounds," "shillings," "pence," and "farthings" remained the familiar terms of their currency. But while in England a system of barter had several centuries before given way to a money economy, in the rude conditions prevailing in the new world a return to this system of exchange was necessary. In the almost complete absence of coin, substitutes for money had to be found and their use regulated by law, in provisions prescribing the form in which taxes might be paid and the manner in which the obligation of debtor to creditor could be lawfully satisfied. These two classes of enactment were then often found together. From this necessity and the resulting legislation seems to have grown the doctrine that such medium only was a legal-tender as had had that quality expressly conferred upon it—a doctrine which was applied later to coin, as well as to substitutes adopted temporarily as a means of meeting obligations which nominally imported the transfer of money units.

These substitutes were of two main kinds: commodities, varying with different communities of the new country, and bills of credit or notes issued by the governments of the separate colonies. Besides these media, Massachusetts boldly and in the face of the law attempted to have a mint and to provide a metallic currency of her own. An account of the experiment with each of these substitutes will now be given.

It should be first noticed that the system referred to as one of barter was not such in the sense that goods were exchanged against goods, but certain commodities were accepted as the best substitute for a medium of exchange

---

[1] FELT, *An Historical Account of Massachusetts Currency*, p. 13. It will be recalled that at this time the English government was struggling with the difficulties of a greatly debased and also underrated silver currency, and consequent scarcity of silver in circulation. Hence one of the great objections to the departure of the colonists was the fear of their carrying coin out of the country.

in the form of coin, and were estimated in terms of that coin; and on such commodities at the estimated rates was bestowed the legal-tender quality and the power of being receivable for taxes.

The most conspicuous of these substitutes and the most universally adopted was the shell money of the Indians known as "wampum."[1] This might almost be said to have been the domestic medium of exchange, while skins of animals were used in transactions beyond seas.[2] But commodities having other uses than those of ornament were soon brought into service, and in 1631 what seems[3] to have been the first legal-tender law of the colonies was enacted by the governor and assistants of Massachusetts,[4] when corn was ordered to pass in payment of all debts at the usual market rate, unless money or beaver had been expressly named in the contract. A little later bullets[5] were ordered to be taken, being rated as equal each to a farthing, though no man was to be forced to take more than 12d. in any one payment in this form. In 1643,[6] likewise in Massachusetts, wampum was given the debt-paying quality within the value of 40s. at the rate of four pieces[7] of black or eight pieces of white to a penny.[8]

---

[1] This was known as "wampum," "wampumpeag," or "peag." It was of two kinds, black or dark blue, and white, the value of the dark being generally double that of the white.

[2] WEEDON, *Economic and Social History of New England*, Vol. I, p. 39.

[3] Virginia may have had an earlier one.

[4] HUTCHINSON, *History of Massachusetts From the First Settlement Thereof, in 1628, until the Year 1750* (3d ed.), Vol. I, p. 76.

[5] March 4, 1635.—FELT, *op. cit.*, p. 20.

[6] *Ibid.*, p. 28; POTTER, "Some Account of the Bills of Credit or Paper Money of Rhode Island from the First Issue in 1710 to the Final Issue in 1786," *Rhode Island Historical Tracts*, No. 8, p. 3.

[7] In 1648 it was provided that the shells should be strung in lengths representing definite values.

[8] It is interesting to note that this currency was subject to the abuses from which metallic currency has always suffered. Massachusetts found it necessary in 1646 to provide that to be a tender it must be "entire, free from deforming spots, without breaches, and suitably strung.—FELT, *op. cit.*, p. 30; BRONSON, *Connecticut Currency*, p. 4.

Similar legislation was enacted in Connecticut[1] and Rhode Island.[2] In Virginia and Maryland tobacco was the commodity most universally desired, and so, in 1633, Virginia enacted that, while contracts, judgments, etc., should be reckoned in English money, they should be paid in tobacco.[3] And a century later Maryland made tobacco a legal tender at a penny a pound, and corn at twenty cents a bushel.[4] In North Carolina corn, pitch, tar, pork were also used at specified rates. Thus, in 1715 any one of seventeen commodities named might be used as a legal tender or in payment of taxes.[5] Similarly in Pennsylvania, in 1719, it was proposed to make various kinds of produce a legal tender, and in 1722–23 a law was enacted making country produce at market prices pay for servants, for imported goods, and for the discharge of judgments and executions.[6]

Thus, in the earliest period of colonial development, the lack of metallic money was made good by the regulated use of commodoties on which was bestowed the debt-satisfying power at definite rates.

At a later stage the foreign coins which came into circulation, though comparatively few in number, were regulated in value and could be used in the same way. Thus, Massachusetts as early as 1642,[7] and Connecticut[8] a little later, made the ducatoon of Holland lawful money at six shillings; and in 1697, under the provincial government, the value of pieces of eight of Seville, Pillar, and Mexico were fixed at

---

[1] BRONSON, *op. cit.*, pp. 4, 7.

[2] POTTER, *op. cit.*, pp. 3, 15.

[3] RIPLEY, *Financial History of Virginia, 1609–1776*, p. 111. See HILDRETH, *History of the United States*, Vol. I, p. 214.

[4] HICKCOX, *A History of the Bills of Credit or paper money issued by New York from 1709–1789*, p. 4.

[5] BULLOCK, *Essays on the Monetary History of the United States*, pp. 125, 126.

[6] PHILLIPS, *Historical Sketches of the Currency of the American Colonies prior to the Adoption of the federal Constitution*, pp. 12, 13.

[7] FELT, *op. cit.*, p. 26.   [8] BRONSON, *op. cit.*, p. 14.

the same value.[1] However, the colonial government was not
given free play in this regulation of the currency in circulation. In 1703, in response to representations made by
residents in the colonies, the home government assumed
control, and the following year a proclamation was issued
naming the value at which the various coins should circulate.[2] As this proclamation was ineffectual[3] it was followed
in 1707 by an act of Parliament in more stringent terms,
providing a penalty of fine and imprisonment for receiving
or paying out coins named at rates other[4] than those therein
specified, although these differed from those assigned by the
local[5] authorities. Whether or not this act of Parliament
alone made these foreign coins a legal tender at the rate
named is a question; but, whatever the result in law, in
fact the proclamation and the act were disregarded.

But the inadequacy of the supply of coin, together with
the unsettled condition of affairs in England in the middle
of the seventeeth century, had led Massachusetts to a project
bordering on treason, if not actually amounting to it. It does
not seem to have been denied that to establish a mint, as
was then proposed, and to exercise the power to coin money
was the assumption of a portion of the royal prerogative.
The plan seems to have been undertaken with the idea
that the home government was then too weak to interfere.
Such a scheme had been elaborated in Virginia some
years[6] before, but had been abandoned, probably because
of the illegality of the plan; it was, however, carried

---

[1] See DAVIS, *Currency and Banking in the Province of the Massachusetts Bay*,
p. 38 (Publications of the American Economic Association, Dec., 1900). The reference
to this act presents an opportunity for expression of acknowledgment and appreciation of Mr. Davis's contribution to a field hitherto incompletely covered.

[2] The values assigned were based on a computation by Sir Isaac Newton, and
were in terms of New England money.—FELT, *op. cit.*, pp. 58, 59. See HICKCOX, *op. cit.*
pp. 10, 12, for effect in New York.

[3] It seems to have been wholly disregarded in the colonies.

[4] Cited by BRONSON, *op. cit.*, p. 26.

[5] *I. e.*, Provincial.   [6] RIPLEY, *op. cit.*, p. 110.

out in Massachusetts, and in 1651 a mint was erected. The currency issued from this mint was appointed to be less valuable by "two pence in the shilling" than English coin, in the hope of thus preventing its exportation. It was likewise enacted that the money thus provided should be the only "current" money of the commonwealth except English.[1]

The establishment and continuance of the mint was the object of jealous notice on the part of the home government, and was one of the causes of the revocation of the colonial charter.[2] This, of course, resulted in the enforced termination of its operations, and with the closing of the mint plans began to be suggested for the use of the colony's credit to supply the deficiency in metallic money[3]—a method followed sooner or later, with disastrous results, by each of the colonies.

This is not the place for a description of each of these experiments; yet an account of the first issue of bills which were made a legal tender by an American colony may not be out of place.

Massachusetts was induced to take this step by the critical situation brought about by the expedition against the French and Indians undertaken in connection with New

[1] FELT, *op. cit.*, pp. 31, 33, 41; DAVIS, *op. cit.*, p. 25. In the chapter here referred to Mr. Davis explains the effect of the mint on the policy of the home government, and also shows the difference between "proclamation money" and "lawful money" in Massachusetts—a distinction which may be applied in the other colonies.

[2] FELT, *op. cit.*, pp. 43, 48.

[3] As early as 1652 a proposition had been made for an issue of paper money in Massachusetts (*Ibid.*, p. 33), and in 1685, when the overthrow of the mint by the home authorities was seen to be inevitable, this plan was revived, and authority to establish a "bank" similar to one which had been formed in London two years before was granted by the president of the colony to "one John Blackwell, Esq., of Boston, with divers others" (*Ibid.*, p. 46). The persons named were empowered, because of the scarcity of coin, the need of meeting the king's revenue, etc., to issue bills on credit (a term already interchangeable with "bank bills" in England, STORY, *op. cit.*, § 1362, n. 4) given by persons of estate and known integrity and reputation, "which may passe with greater ease and security in all payments of twenty shillings or over than monies coined." This organization got no farther than the striking off of bills.—DAVIS, *op. cit.*, p. 7.

York, Plymouth, Connecticut, and Maryland. An attack
made on Schenectady[1] by these foes on February 8, 1690,
had led to a conference on the part of the colonies,
and to an unsuccessful expedition, the expenses of which
were to be met by the issue of £7,000 in bills of credit.
These were at first not made a legal tender, but were
receivable in all public payments.[2] All efforts were made to
maintain these bills at par. Patriotic men exchanged gold for
them, and legislation was enacted declaring that the amount
issued would be limited. They speedily depreciated, however, and two years later (1692) it was enacted that they
should be a legal tender, "pass current within this province
in all payments equivalent to money," and that they should
in public payments pass at an advance of 5 per cent. This
bonus of 5 per cent. was allowed as often as they were
brought to the treasury; and, thus supported, they were maintained at par for twenty years.[3] Issues followed in 1702,[4]
1709,[5] and 1711.[6] Up to the time of these last issues confidence in the paper of the colony had been maintained.
Not only had the bills been a legal tender, but provision
had been made for their redemption at an early date;[7]

[1] FROTHINGHAM, *op. cit.*, chap. 3.

[2] FELT, *op. cit.*, pp. 50, 52. General reference to DAVIS, *op. cit.*, is made. The
form of this first American paper money may be interesting. "No. 2161. 10s.
This indented bill of ten shillings due from the Mass. colony to the Possessor,
shall be in value equal to money, and shall be accordingly accepted by the Treasurer, and receivers subordinate to him, in all public payments, and for any stock
at any time in the treasury. Boston, in New England, December 10, 1690. By order
of the General Court [Signed by committee]."

[3] *Ibid.*, p. 52. These were known as "old charter bills." The taxes for which
these bills were receivable amounted in ten years to about £11,000, and it is calcu-
lated that the issues and reissues of bills during this period amounted to more
than £110,000.

[4] £10,000. Safeguarded by provision for their redemption, and by a resolution
to issue the old bills no more. There was a special tax laid to redeem these bills.—
Ibid., p. 57.

[5] £30,000, to defray expenses of an expedition against Canada. The home government had promised its pecuniary aid in the undertaking.—*Ibid.*, p. 62.

[6] *Ibid.*, p. 63.

[7] One or two years.—*Ibid.*

but from 1707 the collection of the taxes imposed for the redemption of the bills had been postponed, so that the faith of the people in their ultimate redemption had been shaken.[1] At this time, too, the other colonies resorted to similar measures,[2] and there was such enormous increase in the volume of these notes in circulation as to induce a spirit of irresponsibility by its very excess.   By 1712 the notes had so depreciated that attempts were made to bolster them by enforcing or calling attention to their legal-tender quality. The notes of the first issue had been legal tender since 1692, those of other issues from the time of putting them forth, but it was in 1712[3] expressly re-enacted that, with the exception of specialties,[4] they should be a full legal tender.   This legislation was supplemented by legislation abbreviating the statutory duration of debts.[5]   The bills of each colony were a full legal tender only in the colony issuing them.[6]   Nevertheless they gained currency in the other colonies,[7] and from 1712 to 1749 there was what amounted to a single paper currency throughout New England, subject to a more or less uniform

[1] DAVIS, *op. cit.*, p. 89.

[2] Connecticut issued £8,000 in June, 1709. These bills were to be paid out as equivalent to money, and were receivable at an advance of 5 per cent. for taxes. New Hampshire issued £3,000 this same year on the same terms.—BULLOCK, *op. cit.*, p. 207. Rhode Island issued £5,000 in May, 1710.—POTTER, *op. cit.*, p. 7.

[3] *Ibid.*, p. 65. DAVIS describes this as a quasi-legal tender, in that execution was stayed by the tender.—*Op. cit.*, p. 99.

[4] "Specialty " is a contract entered into with certain formalities of writing, signing, and sealing.—BOUVIER, *Law Dictionary*, Vol. II, p. 537.

[5] DAVIS, *op. cit.*, p. 102.

[6] See BRONSON, *op. cit.*, p. 30, for Connecticut legislation making her bills a tender. Also POTTER, *op. cit.*, p. 11, for same in Rhode Island. BULLOCK, *op. cit.*, p. 222, for New Hampshire.

[7] An idea of the situation can be got from the fact that, of the £440,000 of Rhode Island paper in circulation, £350,000 was circulating in Massachusetts, and £50,000 in Connecticut, being of course legal tender in neither place. In connection with the effort, the governor makes the interesting claim that making bills should be classed with coining money as part of the royal prerogative.—FELT, *op. cit.*, p. 115. It may also be noted that there were in circulation £710,000 of private paper which, though not legal tender, circulated at 33 per cent. advance of the colonial bills, and £120,000 of other private paper not a legal tender which circulated at par.—*Ibid.*, p. 107.

rate of depreciation,[1] consisting of notes promising, on the part of the various colonial governments, to accept them in payment of taxes to a specified amount, because declared equal in value to money.[2]

New York, too, had in 1709 joined the procession of those who followed after paper issues. Her first notes, however, were not made a legal tender until 1713, and then the provision applied to subsequent contracts only.[3] These notes, however, and those of Pennsylvania ten years later,[4] seem to have been kept at par. They were not only legal tender, as were the New England bills, but they were safeguarded by provisions for their redemption. Indeed, the New York bills circulated in New England[5] at an advance of from 25 to 35 per cent. over those of the New England colonies.[6]

As issue had followed issue, and, in spite of legal-tender

[1] Massachusetts prohibited the circulation of the bills of the other colonies within her limits (1735), but was of course unable to enforce her prohibition.—BULLOCK, op. cit., p. 209. Connecticut recognized this condition by making the bills of Massachusetts, Connecticut, New York, and New Hampshire receivable for her taxes; and the same thing must often have been done in the other colonies without express authorization.—BRONSON, op. cit., pp. 40, 53. The scale of depreciation was:

> In 1710 an ounce of silver was worth 8s. in colonial bills.
> In 1721 an ounce of silver was worth 12s. in colonial bills.
> In 1724 an ounce of silver was worth 15s. in colonial bills.
> In 1729 an ounce of silver was worth 18½s. in colonial bills.
> In 1739 an ounce of silver was worth 26s. in colonial bills.
> In 1742 an ounce of silver was worth 28s. in colonial bills.
> In 1744 an ounce of silver was worth 32s. in colonial bills.

[2] The following is the wording of a Massachusetts bill of 1737:
"This bill of TWENTY SHILLINGS due from the Province of Massachusetts Bay in New England, to the possessor thereof, shall be in value equal to three ounces of coined silver, Troy weight, of sterling alloy, or gold coin at the rate of eighteen shillings per ounce; and shall be accordingly accepted by the Treasurer and receivers subordinate to him in all payments (the duties of Imports and Tunnage of shipping and incomes of the Light House only excepted) and for any Stock at any time in the Treasury.
"BOSTON. By order of the Great and General "Court or Assembly."
The excepted duties were in this case to be paid in specie, and these receipts were to be used in redeeming the notes.—FELT, op. cit., p. 92.

[3] HICKCOX, op. cit., pp. 16–20.   [4] PHILLIPS, op. cit., pp. 12, 13.
[5] Where, of course, they were not a legal tender.
[6] HICKCOX, op. cit., p. 20.

provisions, depreciation had overtaken the notes; it became necessary in 1727[1] in Massachusetts to regulate the rates at which the notes of the various issues should be taken. In spite of this legislation it seemed worth while to follow this by a stringent tender law in 1731.[2] In January, 1742, further modification was found necessary;[3] it was then provided that silver should be valued at 6s. 8d. the ounce, and that all bills afterward emitted should be estimated at that rate. All debts contracted within the next five years, special contracts excepted, were to be payable in such bills; but if depreciation should occur, due allowance was to be made. Connecticut enacted a similar law the following year.[4] The result of this legislation was that debtors entered into contracts expecting to pay bills, while creditors, when the bills depreciated, demanded specie; and in 1742 it was found necessary to enact that only those creditors who had loaned it should demand specie.[5]

Too much space, perhaps, has been given to this form of substitute for a metallic currency adopted in the American colonies. From the illustrations given it is clear that in the New England colonies, from the time at which bills had first been issued in large sums and at frequent intervals, they had depreciated in value in spite of provisions making them a legal tender and in spite of their being receivable[6] for public dues. It was not unnatural, then, that the attention of the home government should be called to the subject and restraining legislation enacted. The initiative came from

---

[1] For bills issued before 1710 and in that and the following year 8s. were to be taken as equal to an ounce of silver; those of 1712 and 1713 at 8s. 6d.; of 1714 and 1715 at 9s.; those of 1716 and 1717 at 10s.; those of 1718 at 11s.; those of 1719 and 1720 at 12s.; those of 1721 at 13s.; of 1722 at 14s.; of 1723 at 15s.; issues since 1723 at 17s. That is, the last issued were less valuable by 53 per cent. than the earlier ones.— Felt, *op. cit.*, p. 83.

[2] *Ibid.*, p. 86.

[3] *Ibid.*, p. 111. This was known as the "Equity Bill."—Davis, *op. cit.*, pp. 156, 189.

[4] Bronson, *op. cit.*, p. 62.   [5] Felt, *op. cit.*, p. 116; Davis, *op. cit.*, p. 174.

[6] With some exceptions.— See above, p. 58, n. 3. Davis, *op. cit.*, p. 172, well describes the hopeless confusion existing during the decade 1740-50.

London merchants who felt themselves defrauded by the tender acts in the colonies and saw no prospect of improved conditions there.   Already, in 1739, the House of Commons had asked the Privy Council to demand reports from each of the colonies as to the amounts of bills of credit issued and redeemed since 1700,[1] and such reports had been rendered.   And in 1748 the matter was again taken up.   There seems to have been only one proposition made, and that was to prohibit legislation on the part of the colonies making their bills a legal tender.   On February 15, 1749, a bill was introduced in the House of Commons "to regulate and restrain paper bills of credit in the British colonies and plantations in America, and to prevent the same being legal tender in payments for money."   This bill contained an absolute prohibition on the issue of any bills of any kind or denomination without the king's license; it also provided for the subjection of the colonies to such orders and instructions as should be transmitted to them by the Crown; and it applied to all colonies alike.   For these reasons it aroused great opposition, inasmuch as some of the colonies, as Massachusetts, were honestly endeavoring to meet the situation, and indeed had met it successfully, while some had never allowed themselves such excesses as had marked the course of others.   Massachusetts, Rhode Island, Connecticut, Pennsylvania, South Carolina, and New York sent representatives to appear before the committee of the House of Commons and present their arguments[2] against the proposed legislation, and the whole question was finally laid over until the next session in order to obtain fuller information.

In 1751[3] the bill in an amended form was passed.   It applied to the New England colonies only and contained three

---

[1] *Journal of House of Commons*, Vol. XXIII, p. 379.

[2] These were largely constitutional in character, based on the claim that such legislation violated the charter privileges of the colonies.— *Ibid.*, Vol. XXV, pp. 152, 814, 818, 882.

[3] COBBETT, *Parliamentary History*, Vol. XIV, p. 560; *Statutes at Large*, Vol. VI, p. 580; 24 George II., c. 53; DAVIS, *op. cit.*, pp. 253 f.

provisions: (1) The governors should assent to no acts for the emission of bills. This would affect only Massachusetts and New Hampshire, as the governors of Rhode Island and Connecticut had no veto. (2) All outstanding bills were to be called in. (3) Such bills as might be allowed — e. g., sums issued for the current expenses of the colony, for which provision for calling in was made, or sums issued in cases of extraordinary emergency, as war, with the consent of the home government — should not be a legal tender. This measure was to take effect September 29, 1751.

It should be said, in fairness to the colonies, that Massachusetts had already provided for the calling in and redemption of her bills. An effort had been made to persuade the other colonies to agree upon a scheme of redemption. Failing at first in this, it was determined to take advantage of the special circumstances growing out of the expedition against Cape Breton, which had been undertaken with surprising success by the New England colonies in 1745, under the encouragement of the mother country. It had been understood that England would defray the expense of that expedition, and when such proved to be the case, and Massachusetts learned that she was to receive the sum of £183,699 2s. 7½d. in specie as equivalent to the part of the pecuniary burden she had borne (she had emitted £261,700 on February 14, 1745, to defray the expense), after some hesitation it was determined to use this special providential aid to put the currency on a better basis than ever. And so, January 26, 1749, an act was passed with this result in view.[1]   Connecti-

---

[1] FELT, op. cit., pp. 115, 121. A piece of eight (a dollar), estimated as worth 4s. 6d. in English money, was to be given for 45s. in bills of "old tenor" (i. e., those issued before February 4, 1737), or for 11s. 3d. of bills of middle (i. e., those issued between this date and March 4, 1740) and new tenor (i. e., those issued after March 4, 1740). All bills were to be irredeemable after March 31, 1752. The process of redemption was to be concluded by March 31, 1749. All debts and contracts entered into after the time fixed for calling in the notes were to be payable in coin, estimating silver at 6s. 8d. the ounce. The deficit left after using the remittance from England was to be made up by a tax, and the passing of the paper of the neighboring colonies was made a misdemeanor.

cut was preparing to take the same step.[1] The act of Parliament was called forth perhaps chiefly by the condition of affairs in Rhode Island,[2] where a large issue of notes was about to be emitted.

From the date of this act there was a stable paper currency in the New England colonies. The metallic money was still small in amount; but the colonial governments issued certificates of indebtedness bearing interest and payable at the end of a year. Resort was had to heavy taxation in order to maintain them at par, and they constituted a considerable part of the circulating medium up to the time of the War of the Revolution.[3]

The act of Parliament cited did not, as was said, refer to the colonies outside of New England. Up to that time those colonies had given no provocation for such restraining legislation; but after the campaign which ended in Braddock's defeat (1756) their policy with regard to their notes became uncontrolled, and in 1764 the act of 1751 was extended to all the American colonies.[4]

The legal-tender quality about this time was bestowed

[1] BRONSON, *op. cit.*, pp. 68, 70.

[2] The share of Rhode Island was only about £7,800 of specie, as against £183,649 which Massachusetts had received.—POTTER, *op. cit.*, p. 66.

[3] These were known as "province notes," and were treasury notes of the following form: " Received of . . . . the sum of . . . . for the use and service of the Province of Massachusetts Bay, and in behalf of said province I do hereby promise and oblige myself and successors in the office of Treasurer to repay this said . . . . or order on or before the 10th day of June, 1758, the aforesaid sum of . . . . in coined silver of sterling alloy at 6s. 8d. per ounce, or in Spanish milled dollars of full weight at 6s. each, with interest annually at the rate of 6 per cent. per annum " (FELT, *op. cit.*, pp. 131, 141); or " The possessor of this bill shall be paid by the Treasurer of the colony of Rhode Island . . . . lawful money at the rate of 6s. 8d. the ounce of silver within two years from date. By order of the Assembly the 27th of February, 1756" (POTTER, *op. cit.*, p. 95).—See BULLOCK, *op. cit.*, p. 252, for New Hampshire, and BRONSON, *op. cit.*, p. 74, for Connecticut.

[4] PHILLIPS, *op. cit.*, pp. 25, 196; HICKCOX, *op. cit.*, p. 42; 4 GEORGE III., c. 34. The bill was entitled " An act to prevent paper bills of credit hereafter to be issued in any of His Majesty's colonies or plantations in America from being declared to be a legal tender in payment of money, and to prevent the legal tender of such bills as are now existing from being prolonged beyond the period limited for calling in and sinking the same."

upon gold coin by several of the colonies. The expediency of doing so had been discussed in Massachusetts in 1752, and a law to that effect was enacted ten years later.[1] Rhode Island, in 1763, declared that for that colony only gold and silver coin should be lawful money, in terms of which accounts should be kept and debts discharged.[2] In New York a bill was passed giving to certain gold coins at the rates at which they were then current this power; but it was vetoed because it was thought to be in conflict with the act of 1707, by which the value of those coins in the colonies had been fixed.[3]

If the questions with which the inquiry began be recalled, it appears: (a) As to the agent by whom the power was bestowed, that one of the earliest forms of activity of the colonial authorities was the regulation of commodities in which debts might be adjusted.[4] This power was exercised subject to control by the home government, and on two notable occasions Parliament interfered with the exercise of the power: once (1707) attempting to overrule colonial legislation as to the value of coins in circulation, once prohibiting the abuses of the credit of the colonies in the form of excessive issues of bills of credit (1751 and 1764).[5] (b) The power was exercised with respect to commodities at fixed prices, foreign coins, locally minted silver coins, bills of the respective colonies, and finally gold coin at definite values. The reasons underlying these acts seem simple enough. They were, first, such a lack of a medium of exchange as is apt to exist in any primitive community, and, second, the

---

[1] Gold was rated at 2½d. the grain.—See FELT, *op. cit.*, pp. 136, 147.

[2] POTTER, *op. cit.*, p. 94.   [3] HICKCOX, *op. cit.*, pp. 46, 50.

[4] Professor Sumner points out in *The Finances and Financier of the Revolution*, Vol. I, p. 12, that the settlement of controversies at law and the adjustment of debts was one of the very few functions performed by the authorities of the colonies in the earlier period of their development.

[5] Mr. Davis exhibits with delightful clearness the relation of the controversies over these matters to the growth of the revolutionary spirit.—*Op. cit.*, pp. 393 f.

lack of a stable standard of value. This was the period during which the English standard was undergoing a change. It has been pointed out[1] that during this period the silver coins of England had been in a deplorable state, and the great recoinage had failed to meet the difficulties of the situation. The end of the period here considered coincides with the date at which the change of the English standard was acknowledged in the legislation of 1774.

[1] Above, pp. 44, 45.

CHAPTER VII

LEGAL TENDER UNDER THE CONTINENTAL GOVERNMENT

Continental Bills of Credit—Bills Issued by the States after the Revolution.

ON May 10, 1775, the Continental Congress assembled in Philadelphia. The most troublesome question which it faced was that of gathering together the resources with which to prosecute the war soon seen to be inevitable. All was confusion. The treasuries of the colonies were almost empty. Both loans and taxes seemed impossible. No one would lend to the new government yet so feeble, and the citizens of the various colonies were in no frame of mind to submit to heavy taxation.[1]

It was but natural that resort should be had to the financial method so familiar to the colonists, the issue of bills of credit. It was proposed that Congress should issue such bills, making the colonies, now states, responsible for their redemption. In this way Congress would be given the means "of making such expenditures as they saw fit, without asking the previous consent of the states,"[2] and yet the states would be bound to meet those expenditures by taxation in order to redeem the notes. This plan was not adopted without great hesitation, extended discussion, and considerable pressure; but it was finally adopted, and May 10, 1775, Congress resolved to emit bills equivalent to two million Spanish milled dollars, pledging for their redemption the faith of the twelve colonies.[3] The hope that the

[1] On this, see Professor Sumner's interesting discussion, *The Finances and the Financier of the Revolution*, Vol. I, p. 11. [2] *Ibid.*, p. 41.

[3] Georgia was not represented. These bills were to be in denominations from one to twenty dollars, and in the following form: "Continental currency. No. . . . . . "This will entitle the bearer to receive . . . . Spanish milled dollars, or the value thereof in gold or silver, according to the resolution of Congress, held at Philadelphia on May 10, 1775."— PHILLIPS, *op. cit.*, Vol. II, p. 4. The act regulating the issue was passed July 29.—*Journals of Congress*, Vol. I, pp. 117, 174.

colonies would proceed to lay taxes for their redemption of the notes was far from being fulfilled; they rather proceeded to emit bills of their own.[1] But they resorted to other methods supposed to be efficacious in supporting the credit of the notes of Congress. Massachusetts, as early as June 28, 1775, resolved[2] that the bills of all the colonies[3] should be within its jurisdiction a tender in payment of all debts and damages on contracts, and receivable at the public treasury, etc.; and if any one should refuse the notes, or demand a premium for receiving them, he should be deemed an enemy of the country.[4] In August, Rhode Island adopted the same method in behalf of the Continental bills, made them a legal tender in payment of all debts,[5] and declared that any person who should refuse such money ought to be considered an enemy to the credit, reputation, and happiness of the colonies and destitute of the regard and obligation he was under to his country, etc.[6]

It is not intended here to give an account of the various issues of the Continental government. It is only necessary to point out that during this period these issues of the Continental Congress were made a legal tender only by the individual states, though on the recommendation of Congress.[7]

In the same way, when the depreciation had become so great that repudiation, which had been regarded as an impossible breach of faith, was seen to be inevitable, on the

---

[1] Massachusetts, May 20, 1775; Rhode Island in May and June, 1775; New York, December, 1775; etc.—SUMNER, op. cit., Vol. I, pp. 45-7.

[2] Through the Provincial Congress, then the legislative body.

[3] Canada and Nova Scotia excepted.

[4] SUMNER, op. cit., Vol. I, p. 45.   [5] PHILLIPS, op. cit., Vol. II, p. 30.

[6] Similar legislation was enacted by New Hampshire, January, 1777, (BULLOCK, op. cit., p. 264); by Virginia, July, 1776 (PHILLIPS, op. cit., Vol. II, p. 145); by New Jersey, August, 1776 (Ibid., Vol. I, p. 79); by Massachusetts, December 3, 1778 (FELT, op. cit., p. 174).

[7] January 14, 1777. (Journals of Congress, Vol. III, p. 20.) "Resolved . . . . , that it be recommended to the legislatures of the United States to pass laws to make the bills of credit issued by the Congress a lawful tender in public and private debts and a refusal thereof an extinguishment of such debts."

recommendation of Congress the states revised their laws making continental bills a tender.[1]

By the Declaration of Independence the colonies were asserted to be "free and independent" states; by the second of the Articles of Confederation[2] it was declared that "each state retains its sovereignty, freedom, and independence, and every power not . . . . expressly delegated to the United States in Congress assembled." To Congress was expressly granted, in Article IX, the sole and exclusive power of regulating the alloy and value of coin struck by their own authority or by that of the respective states, together with concurrent power to borrow money or emit bills, those bills being based on the credit of the United States.[3] If an interpretation of the extent of these grants of power is to be found in the method of exercising the power bestowed, it may be said that the power to make bills a legal tender was not one of the powers granted, but was among those elements of sovereignty retained by the individual states. "Under the articles of confederation, Congress did not, perhaps could not,"[4] and certainly thought they could not, make bills of credit a legal tender.

It was a power freely exercised by the states during the

[1] March 20, 1780.—*Journals of Congress*, Vol. VI, p. 48. The story of the excessive issues by Congress and by the states, of the measures resorted to to sustain them by regulation of prices, etc., is a familiar one, told in many places, and need not be retold here. Legislation in accordance with this recommendation was enacted in New Jersey on January 5, 1782 (PHILLIPS, *op. cit.*, Vol. II, p. 181) ; in Virginia, November, 1780 (*Ibid.*, Vol. I, p. 302) ; in Massachusetts, July 5, 1781 (FELT, *op. cit.*, p. 194) ; in Rhode Island, June, 1780 (POTTER, *op. cit.*, p. 113) ; and in the other states at about the same time. These bills had fallen about 500 for 1 (SUMNER, *op. cit.*, Vol. I, p. 95), and when on January 7, 1783, a resolution was offered in Congress for their redemption at the rate of 40 to 1, or 75 to 1, it was voted down on the ground that to pay any of the past debts would require " so heavy deduction from the greatest revenue that can be raised as would totally obstruct all present service " (*Journals of Congress*, Vol. VIII, p. 64).

[2] Drawn up in 1778; finally ratified by all the states in 1781.—*Ibid.*, Vol. VII, p. 48.

[3] The consent of nine states being necessary to any one of these acts.

[4] Marshall, C. J., in Craig *v.* Missouri, 4 Peters, 410.

ensuing decade; for, toward the close of the Revolution, in each state there arose a paper-money party, which tried to force on the community a repetition of the experiment so disastrously worked out during the war. Rhode Island, New York, New Jersey, Pennsylvania, North Carolina, South Carolina, and Georgia issued bills during this decade, for the redemption of which inadequate provision was made.[1] In each case the legal-tender quality was bestowed and often there were most stringent police measures enacted, in the hope of sustaining by their aid the value of the bills. Some illustrations may be cited:

As late as 1781 Pennsylvania emitted £500,000 of bills of credit protected by the most violent penalties. The protest of the minority against whose vote these laws were passed is interesting. Eighteen members of the Assembly protested against this action, on the grounds that tender acts were futile; that penalties in such cases were always either unnecessary or unjust; that such legislation showed lack of confidence and helped defeat its own aims; that it was an interference with the rights of private property; that it results in dishonesty and idleness; that it sanctions the violation of contract; that it identifies the depreciation of bills with the interest of debtors; and, finally, that such legislation was directly opposed to the recommendations of Congress.[2]

North Carolina went to the extreme in this direction. By 1783 the paper currency which she had issued at various times in great quantities had disappeared from circulation, and the state was on a specie basis for the first time in seventy years. But there was agitation for renewed issues, and in this year the legislature was to issue £250,000, full legal-tender paper. A tax was levied for their redemp-

[1] Libby, *Distribution of the Vote on the Federal Constitution*, chap. iii.
[2] Phillips, *op. cit.*, Vol. II, p. 189.

tion, and the property which had been confiscated by the state was pledged for its security; but the property was devoted to other uses, the tax was inadequate, and the paper depreciated, only to lead to further issues in 1786, to repeated depreciation, to speculation and loss.[1]

The issue in Rhode Island was perhaps most interesting, because it led to a conflict between the legislative and judiciary departments and gave rise to a decision of court nullifying an act of the legislature. In November, 1782, the difficulties growing out of the issues of the war had been finally settled by an act funding the outstanding notes. But in 1786, after a fierce political fight, the paper-money party again gained the ascendancy in the state, and an issue of $100,000 was authorized to be loaned at 4 per cent. for seven years, after which period one-seventh was to be payable annually. These bills were a legal tender for all debts except those due to charitable corporations, even if arising out of contracts made prior to the passage of the law. A description of the act and its consequences may be cited:

"The law not only created a bank of issue of money, but acted as a general liquidation law. If a creditor refused to receive the bills in payment of his claim, the debtor made immediate application to a justice either of the superior court or the court of common pleas, who issued a citation to the creditor to appear at his dwelling-house in ten days and receive the money as prescribed by law. The judge then issued a certificate of the facts to the debtor, and in case the creditor failed or refused to call for the money within the specified time advertised the facts in the newspapers three weeks, and the debtor was discharged of his debt."

During the following month, June, 1786, another act was passed subjecting such as should refuse the bills to a penalty

[1] BULLOCK, *op. cit.*, pp. 193, 194.

of £100; and in August still a third act reduced the penalties, but attached to the procedure more hateful features than before. Among these was the provision for the trial of the case "without jury, but according to the law of the land." It was on the ground of the denial of the right to trial by jury that the judges refused to take cognizance of the act, and substantially declared it unconstitutional and so void. The law making these bills a legal tender was not repealed, however, until 1789.[1]

The effect of these actions on the part of the states named is written in clear terms in the prohibition on the states found in the constitution of the United States.[2]

By the Articles of Confederation the Congress was given express and exclusive power to regulate the alloy and value of coin struck by their own authority or by that of the respective states. In accordance with this power, in 1782 the superintendent of finance, Robert Morris,[3] was instructed to report a table of rates at which foreign coins should circulate in the United States[4] and a plan for establishing and conducting a mint.[5] In his reply he set forth reasons for establishing a uniform coinage in the country. He said the ideas conveyed by the monetary terms were almost as various as the states themselves. Commonest transactions were intricate and difficult. He advocated the provision of a money which would be a just legal tender.[6]

---

[1] POTTER, *op. cit.*, pp. 118, 131; THAYER, *Constitutional Cases*, p. 73; COXE, *Judicial Power and Unconstitutional Legislation*, p. 235; MCMASTER, *History of the United States*, Vol. I, p. 339.

[2] Art. I, 10, 1.

[3] The Board of Treasury, which had executed the financial policy under the direction of Congress during the war, was replaced by this officer February 7, 1781, and to him was intrusted various and comprehensive powers.—*Journals of Congress*, Vol. VII, p. 29. This officer was again replaced by a board, May 28, 1874.—*Ibid.*, Vol. IX, p. 182. See also Vol. VII, p. 38, for Morris's election.

[4] *Ibid.*, Vol. VII, p. 262.   [5] *Ibid.*, p. 286.

[6] *American State Papers*, Vol. V, p. 101. Speaking of the need of uniformity in coins, as in weights and measures, he says: "Another inconvenience which admits of the same easy remedy is the want of a legal tender. This is as necessary for the

Two years later Congress referred this report to a committee of which Jefferson was a member,[1] and he[2] proposed the dollar as the unit, with divisions and multiples in decimal ratio.[3]　The following year[4] Jefferson's plan was adopted by Congress.　The unit thus adopted[5] was the Spanish milled dollar, containing 385.72 grains of fine silver and 31.75 grains of alloy.[6]

purposes of jurisprudence as a judicial currency for those of commerce.　For, although there is great impropriety, not to say injustice, in compelling a man to receive part of his debt in discharge of the whole, yet it is both just and proper that the law should protect the honest debtor who is willing to pay against the oppressive creditor who refuses to receive the full value." He favored the adoption of the single silver standard, the assumption of the expense of coining by the public.　He suggested a most ingenious method of arriving at a new standard which would introduce harmony instead of added difficulty to the systems of the different states. His plan was to find a common divisor of the sums at which the Spanish dollar passed in the various states.　The dollar was, in Georgia, equal to 5s., in North Carolina and New York to 8s., in Virginia and the New England states to 6s., in South Carolina to 32s. 6d., and in the other states to 7s. 6d.　The fourteen hundred and fortieth (1/1440) part of the dollar would agree with all these values except that of South Carolina, i. e., be contained in them without a remainder.　This he advocated as the unit of value.　The application of his reasoning may be illustrated.　Twenty-four of these units would equal a penny in Georgia; fifteen a penny in North Carolina and New York; twenty a penny in Virginia and New England; sixteen a penny in all the other states except South Carolina, where thirteen pence would be equal to forty-eight of the proposed coinage.　He did not advocate the coinage of the proposed unit, but only of multiples thereof.　He suggested two copper coins, one equal to eight and the other to five units.　The lowest silver coin would be 100 units, equal to 25 grains of fine silver; coins equal to 500 units and to 1,000 units were also suggested. — Sumner, op. cit., Vol. II, p. 36.　See McMaster, op. cit., Vol. I, pp. 196-200.

　　1 Writings of Jefferson, edited by Paul Leicester Ford, Vol. I, p. 73.

　　2 Finding the "general views of the financier sound, but the unit too minute for ordinary purposes."

　　3 Ibid., Vol. III, p. 446.　Jefferson submitted his plan to Morris, who adhered to his own scheme, only agreeing that there should be taken as the unit $\frac{100}{1440}$ of the dollar, which he called a "cent."

　　4 1784.—American State Papers, Vol. V, p. 105.

　　5 Journals of Congress, Vol. X, p. 157.

　　6 Ibid., Vol. XI, p. 129.　On August 8, 1786, it was further determined (1) that the standard of fineness for the United States should be eleven parts fine to one part of alloy; (2) that the money unit of the United States which was, by the resolve of July 6, 1785, a dollar, should contain 375.64 grains fine silver; (3) that the money of account to correspond with the division of coins, agreeably to this former resolve, should proceed in a decimal ratio.　The unit of value thus adopted differed from that designated in the resolution of July 6 by 2½ per cent.　The coins proposed were the mill = .001; the cent (the highest copper piece) = .01; the dime (lowest silver piece) = .10; the dollar (highest silver coin) = 1.00.　There were to be coined the half-dollar (silver), the quarter-dollar, and dime, containing proportional amounts of silver, and the cent and half cent, in copper.　There were to be two gold coins, the eagle = 246,268 grains of fine gold ($10), and the half-eagle.

The issue of copper coins was also provided for, and it was declared that they should be receivable in all taxes and payments due the United States in the proportion of $5 in every $100 paid. The value of the copper coins of the states was regulated and the currency of all foreign copper coin was prohibited throughout the United States.[1]

[1] The establishment of a mint was provided for by a resolution of October 16, 1786 (*Journals of Congress*, Vol. XI, p. 184), but was of course not carried into effect until after the adoption of the constitution.—See below, p. 91.

CHAPTER VIII

LEGAL TENDER IN THE CONSTITUTION

The Convention of 1787—The Ratifying Conventions — Interpretation.

IN connection with the constitutional convention of 1787 there are two subjects with which a discussion of the constitutional aspect of the legal-tender quality of money bestowed by the constitution and that of the borrowing power may be connected: the extent of the coinage power, together with prohibitions of the exercise of these powers laid on the states. As the debates are brief and there is no sharp line drawn in them between these subjects, the whole discussion will be given together.

With the memory of the experiences connected with the continental currency and the paper-money issues of the states fresh in their minds, the members of the constitutional convention assembled at Philadelphia in May, 1787.[1] Very soon after the organization had been completed, two propositions were submitted to the convention as bases for deliberation: the one a set of resolutions referring chiefly to alterations which should be made in the Articles of Confederation, by Randolph, of Virginia;[2] the other a draft of a constitution to be substituted for the articles, submitted by Charles Pinckney, of South Carolina.[3]

Randolph's propositions did not refer to the specific powers to be granted to the departments of government under the system proposed by him, and consequently no

---

[1] The convention, according to the date appointed by the congressional resolution, should have assembled May 14, the second Monday in May; but, owing to the delay on the part of the deputies in arriving, the convention was not organized until May 25.—" Debates in the Several State Conventions on the Adoption of the Federal Constitution," ELLIOT, *Debates,* Vol. I, p. 20.

[2] *Ibid.*, p. 143.   [3] *Ibid.*, p. 145.

mention of the coinage power is found in his resolutions. In the sixth article of Pinckney's draft, however, dealing with the powers to be conferred upon the legislature of the new government, are found the following clauses:

Art. VI. The legislature of the United States shall have power to . . . . (3) Borrow money and emit bills of credit. . . . . (9) Coin money, and to regulate the value of all coins, and fix the standard of weights and measures. . . . . (18) Declare the law and punishment of counterfeiting coin . . . . , etc.

Art. XI. No state shall without the consent of the legislature of the United States . . . . emit bills of credit or make anything but gold, silver, or copper a tender in payment of debts.

These two proposals were referred to the convention sitting as committee of the whole, and there debated until July 24, when the proceedings of the convention up to that time, together with Pinckney's draft, were referred to a committee of detail consisting of five members selected from the convention by ballot.[1] In the meantime, though there had been no discussion of the coinage or money powers of the proposed government, there had been one or two interesting allusions to the general subject in connection with other powers under discussion; for example, on Friday, June 8, in discussing the advisability of giving to the federal legislature the power to negative state legislation, Mr. Gerry, of Massachusetts, who was somewhat doubtful as to the general power, said[2] he had no objection to restraining the laws (on the part of the states) which might be made for issuing paper money.

On June 15,[3] Patterson, of New Jersey, had submitted still another set of resolutions as a proposal for the new government, and on the 18th this plan was under discus-

---

[1] The committee of detail consisted of: Rutledge, South Carolina; Randolph, Virginia; Gorham, Massachusetts; Ellsworth, Connecticut; and Wilson, Pennsylvania.—*Ibid.*, p. 217.

[2] "Yates' Minutes," *Ibid.*, p. 400.   [3] *Ibid.*, p. 175.

sion. In this connection Mr. Madison said:[1] "The rights of individuals are infringed by many of the state laws, such as issuing paper money, and instituting a mode to discharge debts differing from the form of contract." Since the "Jersey" plan[2] provided no means of preventing this he opposed the plan.

On August 6, the committee of five[3] reported to the convention the draft of a constitution, in which article VII dealt with the powers to be conferred upon the legislature very much in the form of Pinckney's draft:[4]

Art. VII. Sec. 1. The legislature of the United States shall have power . . . . (4) To coin money. . . . . (5) To regulate the value of foreign coin. . . . . (8) To borrow money and emit bills on the credit of the United States. . . . . (12) To declare the law and punishment of . . . . counterfeiting the coin of the United States . . . . , etc.

Article XII contains the prohibition on the states introduced by the committee: "No state shall coin money," etc.

Art. XIII. No state, without the consent of the legislature of the United States, shall emit bills of credit, or make anything but specie a tender in payment of debts, etc.

On August 16 these provisions came up for discussion. The debate as reported by Mr. Madison may be given in full:[5]

MR. GOUVERNEUR MORRIS [Pa.] moved to strike out "and emit bills on the credit of the United States." If the United States had credit such bills would be unnecessary; if they had not, unjust and useless.

MR. BUTLER [S. C.] seconds the motion.

[1] ELLIOT, *Debates*, Vol. I, p. 425.

[2] The Jersey plan was rather for a league of states than a federation.

[3] Otherwise known as "Committee on Detail." As to changes made in this committee, see MEIGS, *Growth of the Constitution in the Federal Convention of 1787*, pp. 140, 180.

[4] ELLIOT, *op. cit.*, Vol. I, p. 226.   [5] "Madison Papers," *ibid.*, Vol. V, p. 434.

MR. MADISON [Va.]: Will it not be sufficient to prohibit making them a tender? This will remove the temptation to emit them with unjust views; and promissory notes in that shape may in some emergencies be best.

MR. GOUVERNEUR MORRIS: Striking out the words will still leave room for the notes of a *responsible* minister, which will do all the good without the mischief. The moneyed interests will oppose the plan of government if paper emissions be not prohibited.

MR. GORHAM [Mass.] was for striking out without inserting any prohibition. If the words stand, they may suggest and lead to the measure.

MR. MASON [Va.] had doubts on the subject. Congress, he thought, would not have the power unless it was expressed. Though he had a mortal hatred to paper money, yet, as he could not foresee all emergencies, he was unwilling to tie the hands of the legislature. He observed that the late war could not have been carried on had such a prohibition existed.

MR. GORHAM: The power, as far as it will be necessary or safe, is involved in that of borrowing.

MR. MERCER [Md.] was a friend to paper money, though in the present state and temper of America he should neither propose nor approve of such a measure. He was consequently opposed to a prohibition of it altogether. It will stamp suspicion on the government to deny it discretion on this point. It was impolitic also to excite the opposition of all those who were friends to paper money. The people of property would be sure to be on the side of the plan, and it was impolitic to purchase their further attachment with the loss of the opposite class of citizens.

MR. ELLSWORTH [Conn.] thought this a favorable moment to shut and bar the door against paper money. The mischiefs of the various experiments which had been made were now fresh in the public mind, and had excited the disgust of all the respectable part of America. By withholding the power from the new government, more friends of influence would be gained to it than by almost anything else. Paper money can in no case be necessary. Give the government credit, and other resources will offer. The power may do harm, never good.

MR. RANDOLPH [Va.], notwithstanding his antipathy to paper money, could not agree to strike out the words, as he could not foresee all the occasions that might arise.

MR. WILSON [Pa.]: It will have a most salutary influence on the credit of the United States, to remove the possibility of paper money. This expedient can never succeed while its mischiefs are remembered ; and, as long as it can be resorted to, it will be a bar to other resources.

MR. BUTLER [S. C.] remarked, that paper was a legal tender in no country in Europe. He was urgent for disarming the government of such a power.

MR. MASON [Va.] was still averse to tying the hands of the legislature *altogether*. If there was no example in Europe, as just remarked, it might be observed on the other side, that there was none in which the government was restrained on this head.

MR. READ [Del.] thought the words, if not struck out, could be as alarming as the mark of the beast in Revelation.

MR. LANGDON [N. H.] had rather reject the whole plan than retain the three words, "and emit bills."

On the motion for striking out the vote stood nine yeas to two noes.[1] The clause as amended was then adopted.

On the next day the twelfth clause of the same section was amended so as to secure securities, as well as coin, of the United States against counterfeiting, and so adopted.[2]

On August 28, article XII was taken up. As proposed by the committee of five it read: "No state shall coin money; nor grant letters of marque and reprisal; nor enter into any treaty, alliance, or confederation; nor grant any title of nobility." Article XIII read: "No state, without the consent of the legislature of the United States, shall emit bills of credit, or make anything but specie a tender in payment of debts; lay imposts, or duties on imports. . . . ."[3]

---

[1] *Yea:* New Hampshire, Massachusetts, Connecticut, Pennsylvania, Delaware, Virginia, North Carolina, South Carolina, Georgia — 9. *No:* New Jersey and Maryland—2.—ELLIOT, *op. cit.*, Vol. I, p. 245; Vol. V, p. 435. "The vote in the affirmative by Virginia was occasioned by the acquiescence of Mr. Madison, who became satisfied that striking out the words would not disable the government from the use of public notes, as far as they were safe and proper, and would only cut off the pretext for a *paper currency*, and particularly for making the bills a *tender* either for public or private debts."

[2] *Ibid.*, Vol. I, p. 246.   [3] *Ibid.*, p. 229.

Mr. Wilson [Pa.] and Mr. Sherman [Conn.] moved[1] to insert after "coin money" in article XII the words, "nor emit bills of credit, nor make anything but gold and silver a tender in payment of debts," making the prohibition absolute, instead of making the measures allowable as in the thirteenth article, with the *consent of the legislature of the United States.*

Mr. Gorham [Mass.] thought the purpose would be as well secured by the provision of article XIII, which makes the consent of the general legislature necessary; and that in that mode no opposition would be excited, whereas an absolute prohibition of paper money would rouse the most desperate opposition from its partisans.

Mr. Sherman thought this a favorable crisis for crushing paper money. If the consent of the legislature could authorize emissions of it, the friends of paper money would make every exertion to get into the legislature in order to license it.

The question being divided on the first part, "nor emit bills of credit," eight states voted aye,[2] one state voted no,[3] and one was divided.[4] The second part of the amendment, "nor make anything but gold and silver a tender in payment of debts," was unanimously agreed to,[5] eleven states being present.[6] The various clauses of the twelfth and thirteenth articles, as announced, were then adopted.

On September 8, a committee of revision consisting of five members of the convention was appointed to revise the style of and arrange the articles agreed to by the house.[7] This committee consisted of Mr. Johnston, Mr. Hamilton, Mr. Gouverneur Morris, Mr. Madison, and Mr. King — and reported on the 12th a revised draft of the constitution.[8] In this draft, the clauses referring to the coinage power are found in the form and order finally adopted, that is, as the

---

[1] *Ibid.*, Vol. V, p. 484.

[2] *Aye*: New Hampshire, Massachusetts, Connecticut, Pennsylvania, Delaware, North Carolina, South Carolina, Georgia—8.

[3] *No*—Virginia.

[4] *Divided*—Maryland.

[5] *Ibid.*, p. 485.

[6] *Ibid.*, Vol. I, p. 271.

[7] *Ibid.*, p. 295.

[8] *Ibid.*, p. 298.

second, fifth, and sixth clauses of section 8, under article I.
The prohibition on the states is found as in the final form in
section 10 of article I.[1]

The form as finally adopted then read as follows:

Art. I. . . . . Sec. 8. The Congress . . . . shall have power
. . . . (2) To borrow money on the credit of the United States.
. . . . (5) To coin money, regulate the value thereof, and of foreign
coin, and fix the standard of weights and measures. (6) To provide for the punishment of counterfeiting the securities and current
coin of the United States.

Art. II. . . . . Sec. 10. No state shall coin money nor emit
bills of credit nor make anything but gold and silver coin a tender
in payment of debts, nor . . . . , etc.

Such was the action of the convention.

A review of the proceedings in the federal convention
leads at once to an inquiry as to those in the conventions of
the several states in which the constitution thus drawn up
and submitted to the people through congress was, in accordance with Article VII, and with the resolution of Congress,[2]
finally ratified. Little information as to the grant of power
to the federal legislature, however, can be obtained from
their discussion. The prohibition on the states attracted
all the attention given to the question of the currency under
the proposed government.

For example, in the North Carolina convention, a question of controlling influence was as to the effect of the proposed constitution on the paper issues of that state, to which
resort had been had in the years 1783–86, and which had
been made full legal tender.[3] So in the Virginia convention,
on June 8, 1788,[4] and on August 6,[5] the prohibition on the

---

[1] Section 10 was further amended, but not so as to affect the subject under discussion, on September 14.—ELLIOT, op. cit., Vol. I, p. 311.

[2] For congressional resolution submitting the constitution to the legislature
the several states, see Ibid., p. 319.

[3] BULLOCK, op. cit., p. 195; ELLIOT, op. cit., Vol. IV, pp. 182–6.

[4] Ibid., Vol. III, p. 179.   [5] Ibid., p. 376.

states comes up for discussion and eulogy; but the grant of power to Congress is passed over in silence. In South Carolina[1] only is there a reference to the federal power; and there not such a discussion as to throw light on the question of the extent of power. On May 20, Mr. Pinckney, after enumerating the evil effects of paper emissions, argued that South Carolina above all states needed the provisions looking to sound currency. She would have an abundance of specie because of her exports. "Besides, if paper should become a necessity, the general government will still possess the power of emitting it, and constitutional paper well funded must ever answer the purposes better than state paper."[2]

Three questions suggest themselves at once on reading these proceedings: In the first place, what was the difference between the powers actually conferred on Congress and those that would have been conveyed had the clause " and emit bills on the credit of the United States " been allowed to stand?   In other words, (1) what was the effect of striking out the clause?   And (2) what did the framers of the constitution understand to be the effect of their action in so striking out the clause?   (3) What was the extent of the limitations imposed on the states?   An answer to only the second of the three can be given now.   Answers to the first and third will be found below in the history of legal-tender money under the constitution.

Certain inferences can be drawn from the debate itself. It may be noticed that there were three classes of speakers: first, those who wished to shut out all possibility of a resort to paper money under the proposed constitution;[3] second, those who were the friends of paper money, but recognized the

---

[1] *Ibid.*, Vol. IV, p. 335.

[2] Libby shows a most interesting coincidence throughout in the paper-money party and the anti-federal party.—*Op. cit.*, chap. iii.

[3] Ellsworth, Wilson, Read, Langdon.

necessity in the existing state of public sentiment of placing under control the power to resort to its use;[1] third, those who realized the danger of conferring such power, but feared the alternative of cramping the new government.[2]

It will be noticed, too, that no definitions of the terms used are given. The only hint of a definition or classification is found in Mr. Gorham's words: "The power [*i. e.*, to emit bills on the credit of the United States], so far as it is necessary or safe, is involved in that of borrowing." Just what was the distinction between safe "borrowing" and unnecessary and unsafe bills of credit will have to be discussed in another connection. Attention is simply called now to Mr. Gorham's classification.

Notice may also be given to certain differences of opinion as to the effect of their action on the part of the speakers. It will be remembered that the theory upon which the government was established was that of a government of limited powers. Those powers only were to be possessed which were by express grant or necessary implication conferred. Mr. Mason, therefore, thought the power would not be possessed unless expressly granted; Mr. Morris thought that if the words were stricken out there would still be room for the notes of a responsible minister; while Madison, in the note cited, expresses the opinion, which led him to cast the decisive vote in the Virginia delegation, that by striking out the clause the pretext of a paper currency would be cut off, while the government would still have the power to issue government notes so far as they would be safe and proper. Indeed, "nothing very definite can be inferred from this record" as to the views of the members of the convention.[3] Certainly it is not fair to say,

---

[1] Mercer.   [2] Randolph, Morris, Madison.

[3] E. J. JAMES, "The Legal-Tender Decisions," *American Economic Association*, Vol. III, p. 67.

as Mr. Bancroft says,[1] that "each and all [the speakers] understood the vote to be a denial to the legislature of the United States of the power to emit paper money," although this was indeed the view of some members other than those who shared in the debate.

Luther Martin, for example, in his address to the House of Delegates of the Maryland legislature,[2] expresses the following views: "By the original articles of confederation the Congress have power to borrow money and emit bills on the credit of the United States, agreeable to which was the report upon this system as made by the committee of detail. When we came to this part of the report a motion was made to strike out the words 'emit bills of credit.' Against this motion we urged that it would be improper to deprive the Congress of that power; that it would be a novelty unprecedented to establish a government which should not have such authority; that it would be impossible to look forward into futurity so far as to decide that events might not happen that should render the exercise of such a power absolutely necessary; and that we doubted whether if a war should take place it would be possible for this country to defend itself without resort to paper credit, in which case there would be a necessity of becoming a prey to our enemies or violating the constitution of our government; and that, considering that our government would be principally in the hands of the wealthy, there could be little reason to fear an abuse of the power by an unnecessary or injurious exercise of it. But . . . . a majority of the convention, being wise beyond every event, and being willing to risk any political evil rather *than admit the idea of a paper emission in any possible case*, refused to trust the

---

[1] *Plea for the Constitution, Wounded in the House of its Guardians*, p. 49. There is no question of their views as to granting the power to the states. It will be clear from the debate that they were afraid to go quite so far with the federal government.

[2] Elliot, *op. cit.*, Vol. I, p. 369.

authority to a government to which they were lavishing the most unlimited powers of taxation, and to the mercy of which they were willing blindly to trust the liberty and property of the citizens of every state in the Union; and they erased that clause from the system."

Hamilton, on the other hand, says in his " Letter to Congress," December 14, 1790:[1] " The emitting of paper money by authority of the government is wisely prohibited to the individual states by the national constitution; and the spirit of that prohibition ought not to be disregarded by the government of the United States "— showing that he believed the power to be in Congress.

The interesting feature about the discussion is the absence of emphasis laid upon the legal-tender question;[2] and this seems the more remarkable when a prohibition in that regard had been twice used by Parliament as a remedy for difficulties growing out of excessive resort to paper issues, difficulties identical with those through which the states had just passed.   There was no question about the states;[3] all power in this direction was to be surrendered by them;[4] but, as to the federal legislature, the reasoning seems to have amounted to this: to prohibit the legal-tender quality being attached to bills of credit implies that such bills will be emitted; but it is not desirable that such bills be emitted; nor is it expedient to go to the extreme of saying that they never shall be put forth.   Silence on the subject is, therefore, the safest policy.   Thus, the clause granting to Congress the power

---

[1] *American State Papers*, Vol. V, p. 71.

[2] This is pointed out by PROFESSOR THAYER, " Legal Tender," *Harvard Law Review*, Vol. I, p. 74.

[3] Although the vote was not unanimous on this question — 8½ to 1½.— See *Federalist*, Nos. 42, 44.

[4] Mr. Bancroft's statement that the convention " shut and barred the door " and " crushed " paper money is quite true if applied to the states. He is quoting Roger Sherman, who spoke on this question August 28.—*Plea for the Constitution, etc.*, p. 51; ELLIOT, *Debates*, Vol. V, p. 434.

to emit bills was stricken out, and no prohibition was laid. Silence as to that was maintained; and all that can be said as to the interpretation of that silence is that, although there was a strong and well-nigh universal dread of paper issues, there was a stronger dread of too narrowly limiting the powers of the new legislature; and that there was neither a very definite nor a unanimous opinion as to the effect of striking out the clause, or as to the extent of the power granted.

CHAPTER IX

METALLIC MONEY

Legislation of 1792— Foreign Coins— Standard of Gold Coins Changed, 1837— Subsidiary Silver Coins, 1853 —" Demonetization " of Silver, 1873.

UP to this point in the discussion it has seemed best to separate the story of the American experience on the basis of political changes, which has meant a chronological division; that principle of division will not, however, prove satisfactory in treating of the action the federal goverment since organized under the constitution. The following chapters will therefore be framed on a topical basis. First will be described those forms of metallic money on which the legal-tender quality was bestowed; the resort to the use of bills by the federal government and the bestowal upon them of this quality of being a legal tender "in all debts, public and private," will then demand attention; and, finally, the notes of the United States banks and those of banks organized under state charters which have possessed the quality to any extent will then be discussed. To each of these topics a chapter will be devoted. Within the chapters the plan of treatment will again be chiefly chronological.

Before proceeding to a review of the exercise of this power in connection with the metallic money of the country, some of the results of the investigation may be called to mind. It will be remembered that under the English system the coinage power, a portion of the royal prerogative, included the power of altering the legal value of the coins of the realm without altering the amount or standard fineness of the metal of which they were composed; or of altering the amount of metal or its standard fineness without making any change in the legal value. In each case the legal-tender quality of the changed coin resulted from the authoritative act.

In this country no coins had been minted, except for a short time in Massachusetts; but the power to bestow the legal-tender quality upon money, or upon substitutes for money, had been assumed by the c⌐ ⌐nies, subject to regulation by Parliament. And only those media of exchange possessed the quality upon which it was expressly bestowed.

Under the Articles of Confederation the individual commonwealths only had exercised the power, and they had done so with reference not only to coin, but also to their own bills of credit and to those of the Confederation. Under the stress of the experiences in connection with these bills they had denuded themselves by the constitution of the power to make anything other than gold or silver coin a tender, as well as of the power to issue bills at all. They had set up, co-ordinate in dignity and power with themselves, another government, limited as to the sphere of its powers, but sovereign within that sphere, upon which had been bestowed the power "to coin money and regulate the value thereof and of foreign coin." Such powers as were expressly bestowed upon this government were bestowed in the terms of constitutional law familiar at that time. The power to "coin money" might well be understood to include the power to make such coin a legal tender. This was the interpretation put upon that clause by the first legislation enacted under it.

The new government was organized under the constitution in 1789. Congress met on March 4[1] of that year. On April 15, 1790,[2] Hamilton was asked to report to the House of Representatives plans for the establishment of a mint and the means of securing a currency. His report was made to the House on the 28th of January, 1791,[3] and to the Senate

---

[1] *Annals of Congress*, Vol. I, p. 15.   [2] *Ibid.*, Vol. II, p. 1530.
[3] *American State Papers*, Vol. V, p. 91.

on February 7. It was there referred to a committee. On December 26 a bill was reported, and passed the Senate on January 12, 1792, and, with unimportant amendments affecting only the outward appearance of the coins proposed, was agreed to by the House on March 24 and became a law April 2.[1] This bill provided for the establishment of a mint and the creation of necessary offices. The coins to be issued were described. They[2] were to be of gold, silver, and copper.

The gold coins were to be eagles and quarter-eagles, containing, respectively, $247\frac{1}{2}$ and $61\frac{7}{8}$ grains of fine gold, or 270 and 67 grains of standard gold.[3] The silver coins were dollars, or "units," and fractions of a dollar. The dollar was to contain $371\frac{1}{4}$ pure, or 416 grains standard, silver;[4] half- and quarter-dollars, dimes, and half-dimes contained proportional amounts of silver.[5]

The interesting section, for the purposes of this study, is section 16, declaring that "all the gold and silver coins which should be struck and issued from the said mint should be *lawful tender* in *all payments whatsoever*, those of full weight according to their respective values, hereinbefore declared, and those of less than full weight at values proportional to their respective weights."[6]

In this way it was assumed that, as to metallic money, the legal-tender power was included in the coinage power; and only in 1797 was it suggested that there might be a doubt upon this point. Then, on December 14, Mr. Williams

---

[1] *Statutes at Large*, Vol. 1, p. 246. [2] Sec. 9.

[3] The coins as before were to be $\frac{11}{12}$ fine. The coins designated by the Congress of Confederation had contained 246 $\frac{268}{1000}$ grains of fine gold.—*Journals of Congress*, Vol. XI, p. 130.

[4] As this was legally equal to $24\frac{3}{4}$ grains pure gold, the ratio was 15:1.—Sec. 11.

[5] The copper coins were cents and half-cents, containing 11 and $5\frac{1}{2}$ pennyweights of copper, respectively. In 1783 and in 1796 Congress reduced the weights and the "intrinsic value" of the cent to accord with the increased value of copper. This was imported by government. These cents were not a legal tender.—*Statutes at Large*, Vol. I, pp. 283, 299, 475.

[6] Sec. 16. Nothing was said of the copper coin.

"expressed his doubt as to the power of Congress to declare what should be a legal tender for the states. He supposed Congress had not the power of saying what should and what should not be a tender in the several states. He thought he was warranted in this assertion by the constitution in the eighth section of the first article, in which it was said that Congress should "have power to coin money," etc., and in the tenth section of the same article, in which it speaks of what the individual states may not do. It was evident that the states might make a tender of whatever coins they pleased, provided they did it at the value fixed on it by Congress."[1] No one took the trouble to answer the suggestion, however, and the power was assumed to exist and continued to be exercised.

In the same way the power to regulate the value of foreign coins was exercised by making these coins a legal tender at specified values.

It was the purpose of the act of 1792 to supply a currency adequate for the needs of the country. But, as time would be required for the mint to begin operations and for the coins issued therefrom to gain circulation, it was necessary in this interim to recognize the foreign coins then current and constituting the only medium of exchange. And so, by an act of February 9, 1793, the tender quality[2] was bestowed on certain coins at prescribed rates.[3] The coins mentioned were the gold coins of Britain and Portugal,[4] of France, Spain, and the Spanish colonies,[5] and the Spanish milled dollar of silver.[6] These were to cease[7] to be legal

---

[1] *Annals of Congress*, 1797–8, p. 931.

[2] They were to be a "legal tender for the payment of all debts and demands."

[3] There had been an estimate of the values of foreign coins August 4, 1790.— *Statutes at Large*, Vol. I, p. 167.

[4] Those weighing 27 grains were to pass at $1.

[5] Those weighing 27⅔ grains were to pass at $1.

[6] $1.   [7] Except the Spanish dollar.

tender three years after the beginning of the operation of the mint, and provision was made for the proclamation of that date by the president.

The mint went into operation in October, 1794,[1] but by 1797, at which date, according to the act of 1795, the foreign coins should cease to be a tender, the looked-for substitutes had not been found. It was therefore necessary to suspend the provisions of this act from time to time.[2] Only in 1857 was it found finally possible to dispense altogether with foreign coin.[3]

It will be observed that in the case both of the domestic and of the foreign coin the legal-tender quality was expressly bestowed, and the precedent established by the colonies in connection with their substitutes for coin was followed, rather than the English method, according to which the tender quality flowed from the currency and the legality of the coin. It will also be noted that the legislation is broad enough to cover both cash and time transactions; so that it was again true that the buyer in cash transactions, and the debtor in time transactions,[4] had the power of determining which of the forms of coin legitimized should be used in canceling an obligation.

The question suggests itself as to whether the coinage power thus bestowed and exercised was equivalent in all respects to the ancient prerogative power enjoyed by the English kings. The answer to this question would have been unqualifiedly in the negative during the early years of

[1] *Annals of Congress*, 1796-97, p. 2578.

[2] The president's proclamation of July 22, 1797, named October 15, 1797, as the date for the expiration.—*Annals*, 1805-6, p. 205.

[3] These acts were of dates, February 1, 1798, extending time for three years from January 1, 1798; April 3, 1802; April 10, 1806; April 29, 1816; March 3, 1819; March 3, 1821; March 3, 1823; June 25, 1834; March 3, 1843; February 21, 1857.

[4] There was, however, a great difference between such legislation as this and the application of early English proclamations to cash transactions. Here, there was neither an accompanying sanction to enforce the right of the buyer nor legislation intended to control prices, to which resort had been had in earlier times.

the republic, if the power to exercise is understood to include the power to abuse. While the government set up by the constitution was said to be sovereign within its proper sphere, the doctrine was that the sovereignty, in the sense in which it had inhered in the English kings, had passed to the people, not to the government, of the United States. So much of the right of English monarchs as had been derived from the doctrine of unlimited and prerogative power was wholly without the sphere of federal power. The abuses of the coinage which had been justified by the courts on the basis of this power were limited to the reign of Henry VIII. and his immediate successors. For over two centuries they had ceased on the part of the English government. Until the time of the construction of the Legal-Tender Acts[1] it would have seemed absurd to argue that such a power was included in that granted to the federal Congress by the constitution of the United States.

It was, then, most unfortunate that the first alteration made by law in the metallic coins of the country partook of the nature of a debasement. The disappearance of gold coin from circulation[2] and the scarcity and confused state of the silver coinage[3] required action. As the gold coins had disappeared from circulation because their mint value was less than their market value in terms of silver, this effect could be overcome either[4] by reducing the amount of gold in the gold coins or by increasing the amount of silver in the silver coins, which were legally equivalent the one to the other. As all debtors were at this time meeting their obligations in terms of silver, it was decided that less injustice would be wrought by the reduction of the gold than by the enlargement

---

[1] 1884.

[2] LAUGHLIN, *History of Bimetallism in the United States*, (4th ed.), chap. IV.

[3] The only legal medium actually in use was the silver, "of which there is not a sufficient quantity to answer the ordinary purposes of business."—*Ibid.*, p. 55.

[4] *Ibid.*, p. 71.

of the silver coins. The amount of the gold in the legal coins was therefore reduced by 6.26 per cent. by the act of 1834, and the ratio of gold to silver[1] changed from 1:15 to 1:16. As the market ratio was at this time 1:15.7, the change was such as to overvalue gold, and this method, leading to a charge of having debased the coinage, was not carried through Congress without protest.[2] It was argued, with evident truth, that such a change would impair existing contracts and enable a debtor to cancel his obligation by the payment of less than the creditor had had a right to expect: but the failure to recognize the fact that the change in the market ratio of gold to silver since 1792 had been due to a decline in the value of silver rather than to an appreciation in the value of gold, together with the inclination, which has always seemed to prevail in legislative bodies, to favor the debtor rather than the creditor class, led to the rejection of these arguments and the reduction of the gold eagle from 247.5 grains to 232 grains.

This alteration constituted an unfortunate precedent later on, when, in the opinion of the court in the second Legal Tender Decision,[3] it was said: " By the act of June 28, 1834, a new regulation of the weight and value of gold coin was adopted and about 6 per cent. taken from the weight of each dollar. The debts then due became solvable with 6 per cent. less gold than was required to pay them before. . . . . The creditor who had a thousand dollars due him July 31, 1834, the day before the act took effect, was entitled to one thousand dollars of coined gold of the weight and fineness of the then existing coinage. The day after, he was entitled only to a sum 6 per cent. less in weight and in market value, or to a smaller number of silver dollars." The court goes on to

---

[1] *Statutes at Large*, Vol. IV., p. 799, sec. 1. The gold coins minted prior to July 31, 1834, were to be receivable in all payments at 94.8 cents the pennyweight.

[2] *Debates of Congress*, Vol. X, IV, pp. 4665, 4669.   [3] 12 Wallace, p. 457.

argue that no one would claim that herein was to be found a violation of the obligation of contracts. But the court had not exactly stated the claim of the creditor under the previous legislation. His right was to demand either a thousand dollars in gold or the same number of coins in silver, *as the debtor preferred;* but as a thousand dollars of gold could not be secured by a thousand dollars of silver, the debtor regularly selected silver. It might have been argued that to reduce the gold to a weight corresponding with the market value of silver was not in violation of contracts; but it would be difficult to persuade the fair-minded that a greater reduction than that was not in fact and in morals, if not in law, a violation of all existing contracts.

The need of legislation affecting the tender quality of the silver coins was likewise recognized. It was suggested that the subsidiary silver coins should be a tender only to the sum of five dollars. There was thought to be a question as to the tender quality of copper, and suggestion was made that it should be such for the sum of ten cents; and provision for power to reject coins of less than proper weight was declared desirable.[1]

On June 30, 1832, a committee of the House appointed "to inquire into the expediency of making gold a tender in large and silver a tender in small payments, or the reverse . . . . , and also the expediency of making silver the only legal tender, and of coining and issuing gold coins of a fixed weight and fineness which shall be received in payment of all debts to the United States at such rates as may be fixed from time to time, but shall not otherwise be a legal tender, etc.," reported[2] that they deemed the power and duty of Congress to remedy all defects in the currency beyond question; that the standard of value

[1] See report of Mr. Lowndes for special committee, January 26, 1819; $10 was suggested as limit by report of January 11, 1830.

[2] *Congressional Debates*, 1833-34, Appendix, p. 243.

should be legally and exclusively as it was practically regulated in silver,[1] etc. And while the bill which became a law was still before the House, an interesting proposition was made by Mr. Gorham, who introduced an amendment[2] to the effect that after January 1, 1840, the legal tender for the payment and discharge of all debts contracted after the passage of the bill under consideration should be one-half in silver and one-half in gold coins, which should be made current in the United States, sums less than $5 and remainders less than $5 to be payable in silver.

This act of 1834 was supplemented by an act in 1837[3] changing the amount of alloy in silver coins so that they, too, should be $\frac{9}{10}$ fine,[4] and leaving all coins, gold and silver, full legal tender as before.[5]

Save for the authorization of the gold double eagle and dollar, to be a tender for $20 and $1 in all payments,[6] and of the silver three-cent piece to be a tender for sums of thirty cents and under,[7] no change is to be noted in the law

[1] They recommend a change in the ratios of gold to silver in primary coins to 1:15.625; for subsidiary coinage, to 1:16; and the charge of 1½ per cent. gold and 1 per cent. silver for seigniorage.

[2] *Debates of Congress*, Vol. X, IV, pp. 4652, 4653, 4673. See also LAUGHLIN, *op. cit.*, p. 62. During this debate, too, the question as to the power of Congress which had been raised in the early days of the government was again suggested. "In my opinion," said Mr. Jones, of Georgia, "this government has no authority under the constitution to make anything a good tender in payment of debts. To Congress is given the power to coin money and regulate the value thereof. To the states is reserved the power to make gold and silver and them only a tender in payment of debts. I know that some gentlemen believe that when the value of a coin is fixed by Congress it becomes necessarily a legal tender and the courts will so decide. To this I offer no objection. If such be the legal effect, be it so. If such be not the legal effect, Congress has no power to make any coin a legal tender. If it is the legal and necessary effect, there is no necessity of Congress to do so."

[3] *Statutes at Large*, Vol. V, p. 136.

[4] Sec. 8. The weight of the dollar was reduced from 416 to 412½ grains, the amount of fine silver remaining 371¼ grains.

[5] Sections 9–11.   [6] *Ibid.*, Vol, IX, p. 394, sec. 2.

[7] March 3, 1851. By this act three-cent pieces of such weight were authorized that a nominal dollar (thirty-three pieces) contained only 80/100 of a silver dollar. Their issue was very limited, and was stopped after a short time. By the act of 1853 the standard of these was raised to correspond with that of the other silver coins.— *Ibid.*, p. 591; *Ibid.*, Vol. X, p. 160.

governing the legal-tender metallic money until the reduction of the silver fractional coins to the position of subsidiary coins in 1853,[1] by the enactment of a law the effect of
which was to make gold the only unlimited legal tender in
actual use.

The effect of the act of 1834 was soon manifest in the
substitution of gold for silver coin in general use; and this
effect was greatly enhanced by the discoveries of gold in the
last years of the decade 1840–50 and the great increase in the
supply of that metal during the next few years. No silver
dollars had been coined between 1806 and 1836, and few of
them after that;[2] but with gold so overvalued in relation to
silver, the fractional coins, containing, as they did, proportional amounts of silver, were driven out of circulation.[3]
To meet this situation, it was determined to reduce the fractional silver coins wholly to a "subservient" position[4] by
reducing the amount of pure metal in them below the
proportional amount.

A bill having this object in view passed the Senate March
30, 1852.[5] It provided for the reduction of the half-dollar
from 206¼ to 192 grains, and the other coins in proportion.
These coins were to be a legal tender for amounts not
exceeding $5.[6] No mention was made of silver dollars, but
there were few, almost none, in circulation, and they were at
a premium. This bill went to the House on May 3, 1852,[7]
and was reported back from the Committee on Ways and
Means with amendments on the following February 1.[8]

---

[1] February 21, 1853.   [2] LAUGHLIN, op. cit., p. 69.

[3] A gold dollar would bring only 357.25 grains of silver as bullion in 1853; in
other words, the silver dollar was worth 104 cents in gold.—See memorial from New
Jersey, Globe, Thirty-second Congress, 2d Sess., p. 630.

[4] See Mr. Dunham's speech, Appendix, Ibid., p. 190.

[5] Having been introduced March 8.—Ibid., p. 694.

[6] Secs. 1 and 2. This limit was raised to $10 by act of June 9, 1879.—Statutes at
Large, Vol. XXI, p. 7.

[7] Globe, Thirty-second Congress, 2d Sess., pp. 512, 1235.

[8] Ibid., p. 458.

Among the amendments suggested by the committee was one substituting for the limited legal-tender quality receivability for public dues. The object of this provision being simply to make the coins then provided generally acceptable, the amendment was urged[1] as being adequate for that purpose. It was argued that the Senate provision would not only give the currency required, but would make these coins the standard for the smaller transactions, whereas it was desired to have them "purely subservient." This amendment, together with the others offered by the committee, was lost, and the bill passed in the form in which it left the Senate.

The result of this legislation was the accomplishment of the purpose had in view by those instrumental in its enactment. Gold became the sole medium for the payment of large sums; the silver dollar, being undervalued,[2] was not in circulation; the overvalued subsidiary silver coins served for small payments until 1862, when, by the introduction of depreciated paper money, both gold and subsidiary silver coins were driven out of circulation, and the country was put for a number of years on a paper basis.[3]

In 1873, although no coin was in circulation, the laws governing the coinage of money were codified, and the conditions of law and fact then existing were recognized.[4] By the act then passed it was provided that the gold coins of the country should be a one-dollar piece,[5] weighing 25.8 grains, which should be the "unit of value,"[6] a quarter-

---

[1] Mr. Dunham's speech.—*Globe*, Thirty-second Congress, 2d Sess., Appendix, p. 190.

[2] The silver dollar remained worth 103 or 104 cents in gold up to the time of the Civil War.—LAUGHLIN, *op. cit.*, p. 86.

[3] Until the resumption of specie payments, January 1, 1879.

[4] *Statutes at Large*, Vol. XVII, p. 424, sec. 14.

[5] By act of September 26, 1890, the one-dollar and three-dollar and three-cent pieces were no longer to be coined.—*Ibid.*, Vol. XXVI, p. 485.

[6] By section 9 of the act of 1792 the silver dollar (then equal to 416 grains of standard silver) had been declared the unit.

eagle ($2.50), a three-dollar piece ($3),[1] a half-eagle ($5), an eagle ($10), and a double-eagle—all of which were to be a full legal tender in all payments, at their nominal values, when not below the limit of tolerance. The subsidiary silver coins recognized by the act were the trade dollar,[2] the half-dollar, weighing $12\frac{1}{2}$ grains of silver, the quarter-dollar, and the dime—all of which were to be legal tender, to the amount of $5 [3]—and the five-cent, three-cent, and one-cent pieces of baser metal, which were legal tender for payments not exceeding twenty-five cents.

These provisions were followed by a prohibition:[4] No coins other than those enumerated and described, whether gold, silver, or of the minor coinage, were to be issued from the mint. The silver dollar of $412\frac{1}{2}$ grains had not been mentioned. Its coinage was therefore prohibited. Nothing was said of its legal-tender quality. Whether the effect of this act was to deprive it of the debt-paying power has been the subject of controversy. If the principle of interpretation be assumed that the enumeration of some is the exclusion of others,[5] the silver dollar was by implication deprived of the legal-tender quality at the same time that it was expressly deprived of the character of being the unit of value.

There has been no authoritative construction of this portion of the act, and it is difficult to imagine how there could have been such construction. Such dollars as were in existence were at a premium, and were too few in number to become a nuisance, so that the circumstances would have

---

[1] See note 5, p. 96.

[2] Four hundred and twenty grains of standard silver. The coin was intended solely for trade in the Orient. Its being made a legal tender was a mistake, and by resolution of July 22, 1876, par. 2, this was remedied. By act of February 19, 1887, its coinage was ordered stopped after the expiration of six months.—*Statutes at Large*, Vol. XIX, p. 215, par. 2; Vol. XXIV, p. 635, par. 4.

[3] Raised to $10 by act of June 9, 1879.—*Ibid.*, Vol. XXI, p. 7, sec. 3.   [4] Sec. 17.

[5] *Expressio unius est exclusio alterius.*—*American and English Encyclopedia of Law*, Vol. XXIII, p. 446.

been peculiar under which a creditor would refuse them.
And yet, as a theoretical question, arguments may be advanced
to show that the effect of the act was to remove the dollar
from the list of legal-tender coins.　The act of 1873 was
entitled, "An Act Revising and Amending the Laws Relative
to the Mints, Assay Offices, and Coinage of the United States."
The act of 1792 had been entitled, "An Act Establishing a
Mint, and regulating the Coins of the United States."　The
two acts were similar in purpose, and in similar fashion
enumerated the coins which were to be a legal tender.　Not
all lawful coins were a legal tender.　The trade dollar was
subsequently removed from the list; copper coins had never
been classed among the tender coins.　The later act reads
as though it were intended to be substituted for prior legislation on the subject.　The section dealing with silver coins
particularly produces that effect on the mind of the writer:
"The silver coins of the United States shall be . . . . ,
and said coins shall be a legal tender at their nominal value
for any amount not exceeding $5 in any one payment."[1]　If
these arguments hold good, as the writer thinks, the standard
silver dollar lost its legal-tender power by the act of 1873.
On the other hand, it is argued by the most eminent authorities
that the silence of the act preserved the dollar, and that its
omission from the list left it among those coins which were a
full legal tender.[2]　Certainly, if the act of 1873 had the effect
of repealing only those portions of prior acts inconsistent
with it,[3] this would be the case, as there is no inconsistency
in the silver dollar being unlimited and the subsidiary coins
limited in their tender power.　Such was the arrangement
afterward made.[4]

---

[1] Section 15.　　　[2] LAUGHLIN, *op. cit.*, p. 95; *Globe*, 45th Congress, 2d Sess., p. 640.

[3] Section 67.　"That this act shall be known as 'the Coinage Act of 1873,' and all
other acts, and parts of acts, pertaining to the mints, assay offices, and coinage of the
United States inconsistent with the provisions of this act are hereby repealed."

[4] 1878.

In the opinion of those who hold the latter view, the standard silver dollar, unaffected by the legislation of 1873, remained an unlimited tender; in the opinion of the writer, it lost even the limited power possessed by the subsidiary coins.

In the following year [1] the Revised Statutes were adopted. It was then provided: First, that no gold or silver coins of foreign nations should be a legal tender; [2] second, that the gold coins of the United States should be an unlimited tender; [3] third, that the minor coins should be a tender, as before, to the amount of twenty-five cents; [4] and, fourth, that the "silver coins of the United States" should be a tender to the amount of $5. [5] The question again arises, What were "silver coins of the United States?" If the silver dollar of $412\frac{1}{2}$ grains had been left untouched by the act of 1873, and could still be considered one of the "silver coins of the United States" within the meaning of the statutes, it was now reduced to the subordinate position of the subsidiary coins; [6] if it was deprived of its tender power altogether, this power was not restored by the legislation of 1874.

Unlimited legal-tender power, with authority to coin, was restored, after vigorous controversy, by the act of February 28, 1878, [7] by which it was enacted that the silver dollar, as provided for in the act of 1837, should be coined, and should, with all dollars previously coined, be a legal tender "for all debts and dues, public and private, except where otherwise expressly stipulated in the contract." [8]

[1] June 22, 1874.

[2] *Revised Statutes of the United States*, § 3584.

[3] *Ibid.*, § 3585.   [4] *Ibid.*, § 3587.   [5] *Ibid.*, § 3586.

[6] This the writer understands to be Professor Laughlin's view.

[7] Passed over president's veto.—*Statutes at Large*, Vol. XX, p. 25.

[8] By this exception, which had been tacitly included in all prior legislation, the doctrine laid down in Bronson *v.* Rodes, applying to contracts as between coin and paper money, receives legislative sanction, and is applied to the two forms of metallic money.—See below, p. 126; also the Act of November 1, 1893, *Statutes at Large*, Vol. XXVIII, p. 4.

By the legislation of 1900,[1] which declares that the dollar consisting of 25.8 grains of gold, $\frac{9}{10}$ fine, shall be the standard unit of value, at a parity with which all funds of money issued or coined by the United States are to be maintained, it is declared also that no change is to be construed as made in the legal-tender quality of the silver dollar, or of any other money coined or issued by the United States.

[1] March 14.—*Statutes*, 1899–1900, p. 45, sec. 3, "An Act to Define and Fix the Standard of Value, to Maintain the Purity of All Forms of Money Issued or Coined by the United States, to Refund the Public Debt, and for Other Purposes."

CHAPTER X

GOVERNMENT ISSUES

Treasury Notes, "Receivable for Public Dues," 1812–15, 1837, 1846–47, 1857, 1861—"Tender for Debts, Public and Private"—The Legal-Tender Decisions.

THE power to " borrow money " conferred on Congress by the constitution[1] implied the power to issue obligations in the form of evidences of indebtedness. These might assume either of two forms: that of a promise to pay after the lapse of a definite period of time, with interest until payment,[2] or that of a promise to pay on demand without interest.

In private law, a man who bears at the same time the relation of debtor and creditor to another may, in the adjustment of their relations, use the credit due him to cancel that amount of the indebtedness against him.[3] And, by analogy, there is no reason why the creditor of the government may not be given the right to use evidences of indebtedness in the same way, when he becomes the government's debtor as well as creditor. This principle was recognized in the legislation of 1797, by which evidences of the public debt were made receivable for the public lands.[4]

During the first two decades of the government's existence the admonition of Hamilton was heeded, and no evidences of public indebtedness were issued in such form as to approach the character of bills of credit or to assume the form of money. When the stress of war came, however, it

---

[1] I, 8, 2.

[2] Such promises may be either long-time promises, i. e., bonds, or short-time promises, i. e., bills or notes. Being fiscal, and not monetary, they may be classed together. Compare the English Exchequer Bill.

[3] See article " Set-off," *American and English Encyclopædia of Law*, Vol. XXII, p. 169.

[4] *Statutes at Large*, Vol. I, p. 507.

found in Congress a generation of young men in control who did not know, except by hearsay, the effects of the "paper money" furore in the decade following the Revolution.[1] It was not unnatural, then, that resort should be had to issues of notes by the government; and it is perhaps surprising that they were so gradually adapted to use as a circulating medium.[2]

A loan authorized on March 14, 1812,[3] was taken so slowly that supplementary measures were felt to be necessary. On the recommendation of Gallatin,[4] then secretary of the treasury, the issue of five million dollars in treasury notes was authorized[5] June 30, 1812.[6] These notes were to bear $5\frac{2}{5}$ per cent. interest from the date of issue. They were payable to order, transferable by delivery and assignment on endorsement of the person to whom they were made payable, and redeemable a year from date of issue. They were to be used in paying such public creditors as would receive them at par,[7] and were made receivable in all payments to the government at their par value, with interest accrued to the day on which they were paid in.[8]

[1] This was not true of the president, of course, or of his secretary of the treasury, Gallatin.

[2] In a letter to the chairman of the Ways and Means Committee (Bacon) as early as January 10, 1812, Gallatin says: "The advantage they [treasury notes] would have would result from their becoming a part of the circulating medium and taking to a certain extent the place of bank notes."—*American State Papers*, Vol. VI, p. 652.

[3] For eleven millions.—*Statutes at Large*, Vol. II, p. 694.

[4] *American State Papers*, Vol. VI, p. 564; KNOX, *United States Notes*, p. 22.

[5] The bill was introduced June 12, 1812 (*Annals*, Twelfth Congress, 1st Sess., pt. 2, p. 1490. See pp. 1493, 1495). It met opposition from two classes of persons: those who opposed all measures for carrying on the war, and those who wanted more vigorous measures for that purpose. It passed the House June 17 (*Ibid.*, pp. 1510, 1559), and the Senate June 26 (*Ibid.*, p. 304).

[6] *Statutes at Large*, Vol. II, p. 766.   [7] Sec. 4.

[8] Sec. 6. Section 8 of the act of February 25, 1813, section 8 of the act of March 4, 1814, and section 3 of the act of December 26, 1815, are identical: "That the said treasury notes, wherever made payable, shall be everywhere received in payment of all duties and taxes laid by the authority of the United States and of all public lands sold by the said authority. On every such payment credit shall be given for the amount of both the principal and interest which on the day of such payment may

Nothing was said about denomination; in fact, nothing lower than $100 was issued.[1]

Issues generally similar to this were authorized February 25, 1813,[2] March 4, 1814,[3] December 26, 1814;[4] but they were gradually adapted more fully to use as a circulating medium. The notes of the first two issues were of denominations of $100 and higher; the last two were issued in denominations as low as $20.[5] This rate of interest was convenient for calculation,[6] and the difficulty of transferring was not great; but the need was felt of greater convenience as a medium of exchange. An issue was therefore authorized February 24, 1815,[7] with this end in view. By the act of that date the secretary of the treasury was authorized[8] to use his discretion as to the denominations in which the notes should be issued, and as to whether or not the notes over $100 should bear interest; while those under $100 were to be non-interest bearing, payable to bearer, and transferable by delivery alone.[9]

appear due on the note or notes thus given in payment, and the said interest shall on such payments be computed at the rate of one cent and one-half of a cent per day on every one hundred dollars of principal, and each month shall be computed as containing thirty days." Paragraph 6 of the act of February 25, 1815, is of identical import, though stated in more general terms: "Shall be everywhere receivable in all payments."

[1] KNOX, *op. cit.*, p. 22.

[2] *Statutes at Large*, Vol. II, p. 801; *Annals*, Twelfth Congress, 2d Sess., pp. 96, 919, 1110.

[3] *Statutes at Large*, Vol. III, p. 100; *Annals*, Thirteenth Congress, 1st Sess., pp. 645, 1588.

[4] *Statutes at Large*, Vol. III, p. 161; *Annals*, Thirteenth Congress, 2d Sess., p. 291.

[5] KNOX, *op. cit.*, p. 22.   [6] 1½ per cent. a day on a $100 note.

[7] *Statutes at Large*, Vol. III, p. 213; *Annals*, Thirteenth Congress, 3d Sess., pp. 1177, 1921.

[8] Sec. 3. These notes under $100 were designated "small treasury notes" and were issued in denominations of $3, $5, $10, $20, $50, and upwards.—KNOX, *op. cit.*, p. 38. See *American State Papers*, Vol. VII, pp. 854, 887, 911.

[9] No date was fixed for their payment. The form of these notes was that of a receipt for all dues to the government.—KNOX, *op. cit.*, p. 36. This partial redemption and the provisions for funding kept them from serious depreciation. *Statutes at Large*, Vol. III, p. 144, sec. 3; p. 313, sec. 9. The whole amount authorized was $60,500,000, of which $36,680,794 was issued, $3,394,994 being in "small treasury notes," which were reissued, however, to an amount over $7,000,000.—See Reports of Secretary of Treasury, Dec. 8, 1815, *American State Papers, Finance*, Vol. III, p. 7; Dec. 20, 1816, *Ibid.*, p. 146; also pp. 263, 445, 548, 683. See KNOX, *op. cit.*, p. 37.

It was further proposed to make these notes a tender in private debts.   On November 12, 1814, there was introduced in the House of Representatives[1] a set of resolutions of which the first two provided that the Committee of Ways and Means should be instructed to inquire into the expediency of authorizing the issue of treasury notes which should be the only medium except gold and silver in which taxes could be paid;[2] that such treasury notes, if issued, should be a full legal tender between citizens of the United States, and between them and citizens of foreign states.   The exact words of this resolution may be given: "That the treasury notes which may be issued as aforesaid shall be a legal tender in all debts due or which hereafter may become due between the citizens of the United States, or between a citizen of the United States and a citizen of any foreign state or country." [3]

These resolutions provoked but slight discussion.   By the decisive vote of 95 to 45 the House refused to consider the proposition to make the notes a legal tender between private individuals, and, after a brief debate, they were all laid upon the table "by a large majority."

In the summer of 1836,[4] in the prospect of a large and embarrassing surplus, Congress provided for the distribution among the states[5] of a large sum of money collected as federal revenue.[6]   But the revenues of 1837 fell short of

[1] By Mr. Hall, of Georgia. — *Annals*, Thirteenth Congress, 3d Sess., Vol. III, p. 557.

[2] Compare WEBSTER'S *Resolutions*, April 30, 1816; below, p. 148.

[3] The remaining three were to the effect that the secretary of war should be authorized to purchase in each state, territory, and collection district supplies for the army and navy equal to the amount of taxes due in that territorial division; that after one year the notes should be funded into 6 per cent. stock; that the residue of the revenue of the government after payment of the annual installment of the public debt, etc., should be pledged to the redemption of the notes still in circulation.

[4] June 23, 1836.—*Statutes at Large*, Vol. V, p. 52.

[5] In proportion to their representation in the House and in the Senate.—*Ibid.*, sec. 73.   The distribution was to be in four instalments (sec. 14), of which three were made.

[6] $27,063,430.80.—*Congressional Debates*, Vol. XIV, Part II, Appendix, p. 11.

expenditures by from six to ten millions, and the treasury found itself confronted by a deficit, instead of embarrassed by a surplus. About May 1 of the same year, owing to the great commercial crisis of that period, specie payments were suspended by the state banks, whose notes had constituted, since the expiration of the charter of the Second Bank of the United States in the previous year, the only medium of exchange except coin. In order to meet the deficiency in the revenues, the secretary of the treasury recommended [1] the issue of $10,000,000 in treasury notes. Congress adopted the suggestion and gave the authorization in such a form as to accomplish the twofold purpose of meeting the deficiency in federal revenue and of supplying a medium in which those revenues might be collected.[2] With the second object in view the denomination was reduced to $50,[3] and the rate of interest, not greater than 6 per cent., was left to the discretion of the secretary of the treasury.[4] The notes were to be transferable by delivery and assignment,[5] and were redeemable after one year. By this act no power was given to reissue, and the authority to issue expired December 31, 1838.[6] These notes were to be paid to such creditors of the government as would receive them at par,[7] and received in payment of all dues to the government, including payment for the public lands.[8]

Under the authority of this act the secretary of the treasury issued "a little less than $2,000,000 at a nominal rate of interest (one-tenth of 1 per cent. per annum); nearly $3,000,000 at 3 per cent.; and the rest at 5 per cent." [9] During the year 1837/8, six out of ten millions of revenue were

[1] *Ibid.*, p. 13.   [2] *Statutes at Large*, Vol. V, p. 201.

[3] Section 1.   See action of Senate on Benton's motion to raise their denomination to $100, *Debates*, Vol. XIV, Part II, pp. 47-9; and debate in House, pp. 1302-70.

[4] Sec. 3.   [5] Sec. 5.   [6] Sec. 13.   [7] Sec. 4.

[8] Sec. 6.   Identical with similar provisions in previous acts.

[9] Cambreling, in the House, May 11, 1838.—*Globe*, Twenty-fifth Congress, 2d Sess., p. 363.

paid in these notes,[1] and at the end of the year the situation was little altered.

It was then proposed to grant to the secretary, within the time during which his authority to issue existed, the power to reissue notes redeemed, for the avowed purpose of supplying a medium in which public dues might be paid and of furnishing a substitute for the notes of the state banks which were still in a disorganized condition.[2] This proposition was opposed on the ground that such notes under power to reissue became "bills of credit," within the definition laid down by the Supreme Court in the case of Craig v. Missouri,[3] and Briscoe v. Bank of Commonwealth of Kentucky;[4] that the power to issue these had been deliberately withheld from Congress and should not be assumed, even when no purpose was manifested of making them a legal tender between private individuals.[5] These objections were overruled, however, and a bill granting to the secretary the power to reissue notes issued under the act of 1837 and paid into the treasury became a law May 21, 1838.[6] The conditions of the treasury and of the general circulating medium remaining substantially unchanged, the terms of the act of 1837, including the power of reissue, were extended to June 30, 1839, by an act[7] which became a law March 2, 1839.[8]

It was recognized that both fiscal and monetary objects were sought by the issue of these notes; and when in 1840,

---

[1] *Globe*, Twenty-fifth Congress, 2d Sess., pp. 303, 384.

[2] See Calhoun's remarks.—*Ibid.*, p. 386.

[3] 4 Peters, 410.

[4] 11 Peters, 257.

[5] See the debate in the House, *Globe*, Twenty-fifth Congress, 2d Sess., p. 369; and in the Senate, especially the remarks of Preston, of South Carolina, p. 388.

[6] *Statutes at Large*, Vol. V, p. 228. The bill passed the House (106–99) May 16 (*Globe*, just cited, p. 378), and the Senate (27–13) May 21 (p. 369).

[7] Which passed the House (102–88) February 18, 1839 (*Globe*, Twenty-fifth Congress, 3d Sess., p. 189), and the Senate, without division, February 28 (p. 204).

[8] *Statutes at Large*, Vol. V, p. 323.

again on the recommendation of the secretary of the treasury,[1] it was proposed to extend the terms of the act of 1837,[2] amendments were introduced providing that the bills thus authorized should bear interest at a rate not greater than 6 per cent., at the discretion of the secretary, and be negotiable by indorsement only and subject to all the restrictions applicable to inland bills of exchange,[3] for the purpose of preventing their use as a general medium of exchange and avoiding their alleged unconstitutionality as bills of credit. Both amendments failed, however, and the bill became a law March 31, 1840,[4] extending the provisions of the act of 1837, modified only as to the time of redemption, to March 31, 1841. Similar issues were resorted to in 1841,[5] 1842,[6] and 1843,[7] and upon this method of borrowing reliance was

[1] In a statement transmitted to the House by the president with a special message.—*Globe*, Twenty-sixth Congress, 1st Sess., p. 206.

[2] *Ibid.*, p. 211.

[3] *Ibid.*, p. 285.

[4] See *Ibid.*, pp. 285-8, for filibustering tactics of the Whigs in opposition to the measure. The bill passed the House (110-66) March 27, the Senate on March 30 (25-8). For text of law, see *Statutes at Large*, Vol. V, p. 370. Under this act the notes authorized ($5,000,000 in amount) were to be redeemed either at the end of a year or at any time within that period on sixty days' notice. The provisions of the act of 1837 apply in all other respects.

[5] February 15, 1841.—*Globe*, Twenty-sixth Congress, 2d Sess., pp. 93, 108, 109, 113, 150, 165; and Appendix, p. 6; *Statutes at Large*, Vol. V, p. 411.

[6] *Globe*, Twenty-seventh Congress, 2d Sess., pp. 102, 131, 153, 155, 160, 196; also Appendix, p. 23. This bill was introduced in accordance with the suggestion of the secretary of the treasury by Fillmore on January 5, 1842. He answered the constitutional argument by an appeal to Madison's action in signing the treasury note bills of 1812-15. The bill passed the House (129-86) on January 14, and the Senate (21-20) January 22, and became a law January 31.—See *Statutes at Large*, Vol.V, p. 469.

[7] March 3, 1843.—*Statutes at Large*, Vol. V, p. 614. An act had been passed April 15, 1842 (*Ibid.*, Vol. V, p. 474), providing that all notes previously authorized and then outstanding and unredeemed should bear interest at 6 per cent. from time of becoming due until payment. This was thought an adequate provision against a run on the treasury for their redemption. In his report for 1842, December 15, Secretary Forward advised that this provision apply to the notes issued under the act of August 31, 1842, and that the power to issue be extended to July 1, 1844.—*Globe*, Twenty-seventh Congress, 3d Sess., Appendix, p. 46. A bill in accordance with these suggestions passed the House February 20 (111-51, p. 320), and the Senate March 2, without division (p. 386). On p. 185 of the Appendix can be found a statement as to the amount and conditions of issues.

placed in 1846 [1] and 1847, [2] when the treasury was pressed to meet the demands occasioned by the war with Mexico. [3]

Although no issue of notes was authorized during the session of Congress of 1843–44, interesting action was taken with regard to those already authorized. By an act of July 21, 1841, [4] a loan of $12,000,000, reimbursable after three years from the following January 1, or at the will of the secretary after six months' notice, had been authorized, to meet the needs of the treasury and redeem outstanding treasury notes. At the time of the passage of the act of March 3, 1843, there were still outstanding more than $11,000,000 in treasury notes, [5] of which $8,000,000 fell due before July 1 of that year. The loan was resorted to, and $7,000,000 in treasury notes were redeemed. Those still outstanding bore interest at 6 per cent., which was higher than the prevailing rate of interest. [6] The secretary of the treasury, Spencer, in

[1] This bill passed the House (118–46) July 15, 1846, (*Globe*, Twenty-ninth Congress, 1st Sess., p. 1100), and the Senate July 18, without a division (p. 1115), and became a law July 22 (*Statutes at Large*, Vol. IX, p. 39). By it the president was authorized to issue treasury notes for such sums, not exceeding $10,000,000 at any one time, as the exigencies of the government required, with power to reissue, under the restrictions and conditions of the act of October 12, 1837 (sec. 1). By section 2 the president was authorized to issue, if he preferred, $10,000,000 of stock under conditions of act of April 15, 1842. Neither the stock nor the treasury notes were to bear interest greater than 6 per cent., nor be sold for less than par (sec. 3).

[2] January 28, 1847.—*Statutes at Large*, Vol. IX, p. 118. This was an elaborate bill containing within itself all the necessary provisions. By it an issue of $23,000,000 was authorized, together with $5,000,000 under the act of July 22, 1846. It passed the House (166–22) January 21 (*Globe*, Twenty-ninth Congress, 2d Sess., p. 230), and the Senate (43–2) January 27 (p. 267). Notes authorized by this act were to be in denominations of $50 and over, redeemable at the expiration of sixty days' notice. They were to be paid to such creditors of the government as would receive them at par (sec. 4), and were to be "received in payment of all duties and taxes laid by the authority of the United States, of all public lands sold by said authority, and of all debts to the United States, of any character whatsoever, which may be due and payable at the time when said treasury notes may be offered in payment. And on every such payment credit shall be given for the ¦amount of principal and interest which on the day of such payment shall be due," etc.

[3] Of the notes issued between 1837 and 1850 over $50,000,000 were at 6 per cent., $5,000,000 at 5 per cent., and less than $5,000,000 at ½ of 1 per cent.—See Hunter's speech in Senate, December 18, 1857, *Globe*, Thirty-fifth Congress, 1st Sess., p. 68.

[4] *Statutes at Large*, Vol. V, p. 438. See also pp. 473, 581.   [5] $11,656,387.45.

[6] Report of secretary of treasury for 1843, *Globe*, Twenty-eighth Congress, 1st Sess., *Appendix*, p. 4.

order to redeem these, issued others of $50 bearing interest at .001 per cent., redeemable after a year, but purchasable in coin at par on presentation.[1] For this the secretary claimed he found express authority in the act of 1837,[2] which he maintained was not in contravention of the constitution.[3] These issues having been called in question in the House of Representatives, the Committee of Ways and Means was instructed to inquire and report whether the notes issued by the Treasury Department, bearing a nominal rate of interest and convertible into coin on demand, were authorized by the laws and constitution of the United States.[4] On March 28, the committee reported that they were without authority of law,[5] a judgment ratified by the House when it accepted the report by a vote of 89–67.[6]

Again a period of years was allowed to elapse without a resort to this method of borrowing money, and not until 1857, under the pressure of the commercial crisis of that year, were short-time notes issued. All of the notes issued under the act of 1847[7] were retired by 1850, there having been in that act ample provision for the funding[8] of the notes then and previously authorized. The secretary of the treasury, Cobb, in his report for 1857, estimated that the receipts would exceed expenditures, but said that the

[1] Note the difference between these and those of 1837, which bore the same rate, but had no demand feature.

[2] Sec. 8. "And the said secretary is further authorized to make purchases of said notes at par for the amount of the principal and interest due at the time of purchase of such notes."

[3] "The authority ' to borrow money,' etc., given by the constitution, in its terms comprehends every form of loan which Congress may think proper to prescribe; and it is not easy to perceive how this express and unqualified grant of power can be limited or curtailed. . . . . It is submitted that the government is responsible only for the use which it makes of the power to incur a debt, and not for the use or abuse by the people of its evidences of indebtedness."—Report above cited.

[4] Globe, Twenty-eighth Congress, 1st Sess., p. 46.   [5] Ibid., p. 454.

[6] Ibid., p. 460.—See Report No. 379, Twenty-eighth Congress, 1st Sess., House of Representatives. Compare KNOX, op. cit., p. 53.

[7] Except $200,000.

[8] Sections 13, 14 of the act of 1847.—Statutes at Large, Vol. IX, p. 118.

financial revulsion which had caused the banks to suspend specie payment in October had also caused a large part of the dutiable merchandise to be stored without payment of duty, where it could remain three years. In the meantime he recommended that authority be given to issue treasury notes as the demands of the public service should require.[1] A bill similar to that of 1847[2] was immediately introduced into both houses of Congress, and very soon became a law.[3]

As in the case of previous issues, these notes, too, were to be paid to such creditors of the government as would receive them at par, and received in payment of all public dues.[4]

The whole amount of notes authorized by this act of 1857 was issued,[5] and in 1860 there were still outstanding $19,690,500. In June of that year a loan of $21,000,000 was authorized[6] for the purpose of redeeming the treasury notes still outstanding and replacing those which had been received into the treasury for public dues. Under

---

[1] "The exigency being regarded as temporary, the mode of providing for it should be of a temporary character. It is therefore recommended that authority be given to the department by law to issue treasury notes for an amount not exceeding $20,000,000, payable within a limited time, and carrying a specific rate of interest, whenever the demands of the public service may call for a greater amount of money than shall happen to be in the treasury subject to the treasurer's drafts in payment of warrants."—Report of December 8, 1857; *Globe*, Thirty-fifth Congress, 1st Sess., Appendix, p. 6.

[2] Except that there was no provision for funding, and the method of issuing was different.

[3] December 23. Notes not to exceed $20,000,000 in amount, of denominations not less than $100, were authorized. They were to be redeemable one year from date of issue. The first issue of not over $6,000,000 should bear such interest as the secretary, with the approval of the president, should determine. The remaining issues were to be advertised for thirty days, and then exchanged for their par value in specie with such bidders as would make the exchange at the lowest rate of interest, not exceeding 6 per cent. Power to issue and to reissue within the limits of the amount authorized extended to January 1, 1859.—*Ibid.*, pp. 103, 154; *Statutes at Large*, Vol. IX, p. 257.

[4] The provisions in this connection are identical with those of the act of 1847.

[5] At various rates.—See Knox, *op. cit.*, p. 71.

[6] June 22, 1860. Stock was to be issued at a rate of interest not greater than 6 per cent., for a time not greater than twenty nor less than ten years.—*Statutes at Large*, Vol. XII, p. 79.

authority of this act Secretary Cobb invited proposals[1] for a portion of the loan; but before the time of payment arrived the critical political situation so affected the credit of the government that in his report of December 4, 1860,[2] the secretary recommended the repeal of the act of June as to the amount not taken and the grant of authority to substitute treasury notes.[3]   A bill drawn in accordance with his recommendations[4] became a law December 17, 1860.[5]

The amounts[6] thus authorized were issued in January, 1861.   The following month a loan of $25,000,000 was authorized,[7] but it was taken so slowly and at such rates[8] as to demand supplementary measures; and again, within a month,[9] the "Morrill tariff law" was enacted, embracing, in addition to revenue provisions, the authority to borrow $10,-000,000 by the issue either of bonds or of treasury notes, together with the power to substitute for any of the loans previously authorized notes which should be redeemable at any time within ten years from the passage of the act, and receivable in payment for all debts due the United States, and payable in all cases where creditors of the government should be willing to receive them.[10]   With this issue closed the series of issues evoked by the crisis of 1857.

---

[1] $10,000,000 at 5 per cent., September 8, 1860.

[2] *Globe*, Thirty-sixth Congress, 2d Sess., Appendix, p. 8.

[3] Based on the receipts from sales of public lands.

[4] He resigned December 10, 1860.   The bill passed the House December 10 and the Senate December 12.—*Ibid.*, pp. 45, 71.

[5] *Statutes at Large*, Vol. XII, p. 21.   The differences between this act and that of 1857 are very slight.   By it the power to issue and reissue extended to January 1, 1863 (Sec. 10).

[6] $10,000,000, redeemable at the expiration of a year at rates of interest varying from 6 to 12 per cent.—KNOX, *op. cit.*, p. 77.

[7] February 8, 1861.—*Statutes at Large*, Vol. XII, p. 129.

[8] $18,415,000 was the amount issued, at an average rate of only $83.03 on the $100.

[9] March 2, 1861.—*Ibid.*, p. 178.   See also *Globe*, Thirty-sixth Congress, 2d Sess., pp. 998, 1016, 1065, 1201, for the debate in the Senate and House and passage of the bill.

[10] The power to issue was limited to June 30, 1862, and nothing was said of the power to reissue.—See KNOX, *op. cit.*, p. 79.

When Congress reassembled in special session on July 4, 1861, the condition of war had supervened. Mr. Chase had assumed the Treasury portfolio and transmitted his report to Congress on the opening day of its session.[1] He reported that, under the act of March 2, $4,901,000 in treasury notes had been disposed of in April at or above par, while $2,584,550 had been issued after that time either at par in exchange for coin or in payment to public creditors. He estimated the sum required for the fiscal year to be not less than $318,000,000, of which more than $12,000,000[2] would be needed to provide for the treasury notes "due and maturing." Of this amount he thought $80,000,000 should be provided by taxation, the rest by loans such as would appeal to the general mass of the people, as "in a contest for national existence and the sovereignty of the people it is eminently proper that the appeal for the means of prosecuting it with energy to a speedy and successful issue should be made, in the first instance at least, to the people themselves." Therefore, in order to appeal to the people and make the burden as light because as universal as possible, he recommended a loan of $100,000,000 in treasury notes or exchequer bills, bearing a yearly interest of 7.3 per cent. (one cent a day on $50), to be paid half-yearly, and redeemable at the pleasure of the United States after three years from date of issue. These notes were to be issued in sums of $50, $100, $500, $1,000, and $5,000.[3]

Besides these, the secretary proposed the issue of $50,-000,000 in small denominations, $10, $20, $25, payable a year from date, bearing interest at 3.65 per cent.,[4] or, if more convenient, made redeemable in coin on demand, with-

---

[1] *Globe*, Thirty-seventh Congress, 1st Sess., Appendix, p. 4.　　　[2] $12,639,861.64.

[3] With the amount of interest for specified periods engraved on the back of each note.

[4] To be exchanged for those bearing 7.3 per cent.

out interest. "In either form," said the secretary, "treasury notes of these smaller denominations may prove very useful if prudently used in anticipation of revenues certain to be received. The greatest care will be requisite to prevent the degradation of these issues into irredeemable paper currency, than which no more certainly fatal expedient for impoverishing the means and discrediting the government of any country can be devised." [1]

A bill embodying these suggestions passed the two houses of Congress after slight discussion, and almost unanimously, becoming a law July 17. [1] By it a loan of $250,000,000 was authorized in the form of bonds [2] or treasury notes [3] at the discretion of the secretary.

Attention is particularly called to the second alternative suggested by the secretary; for he was also given power to issue in exchange for coin, or pay for salaries and other dues from the United States, treasury notes to an amount not greater than $50,000,000, of a smaller denomination, [4] either bearing interest at the rate of 3.65 per cent., and payable a year from date of issue, [5] *or not bearing interest, and payable on demand,* [6] power to issue and to reissue being granted up to December 31, 1862.

It is an indication of the haste with which the act was passed that nothing was said in it about receivability for

[1] *Ibid.*, pp. 61, 128; *Statutes at Large*, Vol. XII, p. 259. See "Study of Demand Notes of 1861," R. M. Breckenridge, *Sound Currency*, Vol. V, p. 20.

[2] Coupon, or registered, to bear interest not greater than 7 per cent., payable semi-annually, redeemable after twenty years.

[3] Of denomination not less than $50, payable three years from date of issue, with interest at 7.3 per cent. per annum.

[4] Not less than $10, according to this act, reduced to $5 by the act of August 5.

[5] Exchangeable in sums of $100 for the non-interest-bearing notes.

[6] Besides these opportunities for choice as to the form of the obligations he would issue, the secretary was authorized to issue twenty millions, in such denominations as he saw fit, in notes payable within twelve months, bearing interest at a rate not greater than 6 per cent.

public dues, and this quality was therefore bestowed by a supplementary act of August 5.[1]

It appears, then, that up to this time, on five occasions,[2] the quality of being receivable in all payments to the government had been bestowed upon notes issued by the government. In each case the notes had been likewise payable to such creditors as would voluntarily receive them. These notes had varied widely in character, from true exchequer bills of large denomination, bearing interest, to notes of small denomination, bearing a nominal rate of interest or none at all. Resort had been had to these last on one occasion, when all other resources had seemed exhausted, at the close of the second war with England. Here, at the beginning of another war, before any other resources had been tried, resort was had to non-interest-bearing notes wholly adapted to use as a medium of exchange.[3]

With the issue of the legal-tender notes of the war is reached the point at which interest in the whole subject culminates. No precedent for such notes could be found during the life of the United States under the constitution. Their issue brought immediately to the front serious questions of constitutional power, as well as of policy, expediency, and national honor. It is impossible to enter upon a discussion here of the fiscal operations of which these issues were a part;[4] and only so much of the history of these notes will be narrated as is found necessary for the purpose of this study.

---

[1] *Globe,* Thirty-seventh Congress, 1st Sess., pp. 219, 268; *Statutes at Large,* Vol. XII, p. 313, sec. 5. By section 3 of this act the denomination was reduced to $5. By the act of March 17, 1862, these notes were made a legal tender.— *Globe,* Thirty-seventh Congress, 2d Sess., pp. 1116, 1117, 1165; *Statutes at Large,* Vol. XII, p. 370, sec. 2. An additional issue of $10,000,000 had been authorized February 12, 1862.—*Ibid.,* p. 338.

[2] 1812–15; 1837–43; 1846–47; 1857; 1861.

[3] 1815. In 1841, notes bearing but a nominal rate had been issued, but their issue had been disapproved by Congress.

[4] For the history of these transactions see *Report of the Monetary Commission of the Indianapolis Convention* (1898), pp. 398 f.

For the sake of completeness, however, the various acts under which legal-tender notes were authorized will be described.

In his report to Congress at the opening of the session in 1861[1] Secretary Chase submitted estimates for the continuance of the war, which he hoped might be terminated the following summer. Various plans were proposed,[2] but no hint of the possibility of resorting to government issues which would be made a tender in private transactions was found in this report.

Of the issues authorized by the act of the previous July 17, $21,165,220 had been put out in denominations of $5, $10, and $20, which the secretary characterized as "a loan from the people, payable on demand, without interest." These notes, with some exceptions, circulated freely with gold, and were redeemed in gold at the treasury until the suspension of specie payments.[3] This event occurred on December 28, 1861, and on the 30th Mr. Spaulding introduced into the House of Representatives a bill authorizing the issue of demand notes which should be a full legal tender.[4] This was done under the plea of the absolute necessity of the measure. It was claimed that neither a banking system such as the secretary proposed nor the system of taxation which had to be developed to meet the emergency of war could be created without great delay; and the extreme measure of a legal-tender paper money was declared by its advocates the only adequate provision for the exigency then facing the government.

[1] December 9, 1861.—*Globe*, Thirty-seventh Congress, 2d Sess., Appendix, p. 23.

[2] The issue of circulatory notes to replace the notes of state banks. Out of these suggestions grew the national banking system later erected.

[3] KNOX (*op. cit.*, p. 90) discusses these notes, and declares them to have been reluctantly received. BRECKENRIDGE (in the study cited above, p. 166) shows the contrary to have been generally true. See also report of Secretary Chase for 1862, *Globe*, Thirty-seventh Congress, 3d Sess., Appendix, p. 20; SCHUCKERS, *The Life and Public Services of Salmon Portland Chase*, chap. XXVII.

[4] *Globe*, Thirty-seventh Congress, 2d Sess., p. 435. The bill was known as "House Bill 240," "To authorize the issue of United States notes, and for the funding and redemption thereof."

To discuss the necessity of this measure is to weigh it in connection with the whole fiscal policy of the secretary. This has recently been done by one having access to valuable authorities, with the following result : [1]

"In examining the conditions under which the United States notes were issued, we have seen that . . . . it was the temporary deposits and certificates of indebtedness, and not the legal-tender paper long delayed in issue, which tided the government over the trying period of February, 1862, and the following weeks; that the entire issue of legal-tender notes bore a very small and unimportant proportion to the total war expenditures; that Secretary Chase and Congress made grave mistakes in their policy in taxation and the sale of bonds; and that the plans of bankers and of the minority of the Ways and Means Committee, which might have prevented this disastrous step, were proposed and urged upon the government."

In answer to the argument of necessity was advanced the argument of lack of power. This had, of course, been anticipated, and the opinion of the attorney-general had been sought and was quoted by Mr. Spaulding in his exposition of the measure. [2] This opinion must be admitted to be a feeble support, amounting merely to the statement that there was no prohibition in the constitution, which all knew, and the inference that a failure to prohibit amounted to a permission which was contrary to all canons of interpretations. The opinion of Secretary Chase was also sought and obtained, sustaining the constitutionality of the measure. [3]

The measure was pressed as a war measure, a "measure of necessity, not of choice," [4] to meet the extraordinary needs

---

[1] D. C. BARRETT, "The Supposed Necessity of the Legal-Tender Paper," *Quarterly Journal of Economics*, May, 1902.

[2] January 25.—*Globe*, Thirty-seventh Congress, 2d Sess., p. 525.

[3] Letter from Secretary Chase to Committee of Ways and Means.—*Ibid.*, p. 617.

[4] See Mr. Spaulding's speech.

of extraordinary times—the only remaining resource after all others had been exhausted. The power to issue such notes was claimed to be authorized first as an implied power because it furnished a means toward the exercise of the powers "to raise and *support* an army," "to provide and *maintain* a navy," and to regulate the value of coin,[1] expressly conferred.

But in addition to the argument drawn from the clause granting the implied powers, this was claimed to be justified by the simple fact of sovereignty, the broad claim which afterward proved so effective[2] being now put forth. "I am here," argued Mr. Bingham, "to assert the rightful authority of the American people as a nationality, a sovereignty under and by virtue of the constitution. By that sovereignty, which is known by the name of 'We, the people of the United States,' the government of the United States has been invested with the attribute of sovereignty, which is inseparable from every sovereignty beneath the sun—the power to determine what shall be money—that is to say, what shall be the standard of value, what shall be the medium of exchange for the purpose of regulating exchange and facilitating all commercial transactions of the country and among the people. If the government of the United States had not this power, it would be poor indeed; it would be no government at all."[3] Mr. Pike, however, went so far on the other side as to admit that the exercise of this power was plainly an excess of power under the constitution; but he contended that it was justified by the existing emergency, which he found analogous to a case of fire rendering lawful

---

[1] "In regulating the value of coin, either foreign or domestic, Congress may provide that gold and silver shall be of no greater value in the payment of debts within the United States than the treasury notes issued on the credit of the government which stamps such coin and fixes its value."—*Ibid.*, p. 524.

[2] In Justice Gray's opinion in Juillard *v.* Greenman, below, p. 133.

[3] See Bingham's speech, February 4.—*Globe*, Thirty-seventh Congress, 2d Sess. p. 636.

a destruction of property under ordinary circumstances wholly illegal.[1]

The argument against the legitimacy of the exercise of the power thus attempted for the first time was perhaps best set forth in the House by Pendleton.[2] He referred first to the uninterrupted and consistent interpretation put upon the constitution by Congress in never even considering the exercise of such a power: "Not only was such a law never passed, but such a law was never voted on, never proposed, never introduced, never recommended by any department of the government; the measure was never seriously considered in either branch of government." Not only was there no grant of such power, but the omission was a deliberate and purposeful omission, because it was intended that neither in the states nor in the federal government should such a power reside.

The bill passed the House on February 6,[3] and was introduced with amendments in the Senate the following day, when Mr. Fessenden, chairman of the Finance Committee, presented the measure, with a letter from the secretary of the treasury urging immediate action. The important amendments proposed by the Committee on Finance were a provision for the collection of import duties in coin, i. e., inserting in the provision by which these notes, as in the case of former issues, should be receivable for all public dues, an exception in favor of import duties; a similar exception in the case of public creditors, requiring the payment of "interest on bonds and notes" to be in coin; and the bestowal of power on the secretary to sell at any time 6 per cent. bonds at their market value to secure coin for the payment

---

[1] See Pike's speech, February 5.—*Globe*, Thirty-seventh Congress, 2d Sess., p. 658.

[2] January 29.—*Ibid.*, p. 549. But see arguments of Morrill and Conkling, pp. 629-35.

[3] By a vote of 93 to 59. All the Democrats and such Republicans as Morrill, Conkling, Pomeroy, Lovejoy, Rollins, Thomas of Massachusetts, etc., voted against the measure.—*Ibid.*, p. 695.

of the interest on the public debt.[1] The Finance Committee did not recommend an amendment striking out the legal-tender clause, but this was soon introduced on the floor of the Senate.[2] After a debate similar to that in the House, however, the amendment was lost by a vote of 17 to 22 on February 13.[3]

Both Mr. Sherman and Mr. Bayard referred to the probability of interpretation by the Supreme Court. " When I feel so strongly the necessity of this measure, I am constrained to assume the power and refer our authority to exercise it to the court," said Mr. Sherman. " The thing is to my mind so palpable a violation of the federal constitution," said Mr. Bayard, " that I doubt whether in any court of justice in the country having a decent regard for its own respectability you can possibly expect that this bill . . . . will not receive its condemnation as unconstitutional and void as to this clause." The bill became a law February 25, 1862.[4] By it the secretary was authorized to issue on the credit of the United States $150,000,000 in non-interest-bearing notes, of such denominations, not less than $5, as he saw fit, $50,000,000 to replace the demand notes outstanding. These notes were to be " receivable in payment of all taxes, internal duties, excises, debts, and demands of every kind due to the United States, except duties on imports, and of all claims and demands against the United States of every kind whatsoever, except for interest on bonds and notes, which shall be paid in coin, and shall also be lawful money and a legal tender in payment of all debts, public and private, within the United States, except duties on imports and interest as aforesaid." Power to reissue as the public interest might

---

[1] See Fessenden's speech, February 12.—*Ibid.*, p. 763. Mr. Fessenden did not put his argument on the constitutional ground, but on the ground that it was a confession of weakness, "bad faith, bad morals," and that the loss would fall chiefly on the poor.

[2] *Ibid.*, p. 767.   [3] *Ibid.*, pp. 791, 795, 860.   [4] *Statutes at Large*, Vol. XII, p. 345.

require was granted.[1] Holders of the notes were authorized to deposit them in sums of $50, and to receive certificates of deposit, in exchange for which would be given 6 per cent. compound-interest-bearing bonds, redeemable after five and payable after twenty years.[2]

On March 17 an act was signed making the demand notes of the acts of July 17 and August 5, 1861, and February 12, 1862, a legal tender, so that they were both receivable for import duties and a legal tender.[3]

It will be remembered that $50,000,000 of the $150,000,-000 authorized were to replace the $50,000,000 of demand notes authorized the previous summer.[4] On June 7, 1862, the secretary reported to the Committee of Ways and Means that nearly all the demand notes were held at a premium because of their availability for the payment of duties; that the legal tenders had been kept at or near par by the provision for funding them; and that the exigencies of the public service required the issue of another $150,000,000, part of which, he thought, should be in lower denominations than $5, in order to replace the issues of state banks.[5]

---

[1] Sec. 1.

[2] Sec. 3. Bonds of this kind were authorized to the amount of $500,000,000, to be disposed of by the secretary at their market prices in coin or for treasury notes, and to be exempt from state taxation. By the same act provision was made for the application of coin received for import duties as a special fund to the payment of interest on the public debt, and to the creation of a sinking-fund for the gradual extinction of the debt.—Sec. 5.

[3] *Statutes at Large*, Vol. XII, p. 370.

[4] Or, rather, $60,000,000, since $10,000,000 additional were authorized by the act of February 12, 1862.—*Ibid.*, p. 338.

[5] " I am aware of the general objections to the issue of notes under $5, and concede their cogency. Indeed, under ordinary circumstances they are unanswerable; but in the existing circumstances of the country they lose most if not all of their force. . . . . It may be properly further observed that since the United States notes are made a legal tender and maintained nearly at par with gold by the provision for their conversion into bonds bearing 6 per cent. interest, payable in coin, it is not easy to see why small notes may not be issued as safely as large ones. Resumption of payments in specie can be more certainly and early effected, and with far less of loss and inconvenience to the community, if the currency, small as well as large, is of United States notes, than if the channels of circulation are left to be filled up by the emissions of non-specie-paying corporations, solvent and insolvent."—*Globe*, Thirty-seventh Congress, 2d Sess., p. 2768.

A bill introduced into Congress in accordance with the secretary's recommendation passed both houses[1] and became a law July 11, 1862.[2] By it was authorized the issue of $150,000,000 in notes similar to those authorized by the act of February 25, except that $35,000,000 might be of denominations lower than $5, but not lower than $1. Like the former issue, these were to be receivable in all payments to the government, except for import duties, and in all payments by the government, except interest on the public debt, and were "lawful money and a legal tender in payment of all debts, public and private, within the United States, except," etc.[3]

This was soon followed by an act[4] prohibiting the circulation of notes intended to circulate as money of lower denomination than one dollar issued by "any private corporation, banking association, firm, or individual." Such notes had been issued to supply the gap left by the withdrawal of the subsidiary silver from circulation, when the legal-tender paper had depreciated to a point low enough to produce this effect.[5]

[1] It passed the House June 24 by a vote of 76 to 47, and the Senate July 2 by a vote of 23 to 13 (*ibid.*, pp. 2889, 2903). In the House an amendment to strike out the legal-tender provision was lost (June 23, p. 2889), and in the Senate an amendment introduced by Mr. Sherman taxing state banks 2 per cent. on the amount of their notes in circulation was voted down (10-27, July 2, p. 3071). That it was a departure from the pledges implied, if not expressly given, during the debate on the first legal-tender act was not denied. Only Mr. Stevens, chairman of the Committee of Ways and Means, had admitted the possibility of further issues. Mr. Spaulding, chairman of the sub-committee and "father of the legal tenders," admitted the desperate nature of the situation. "Paper credit in some form must be issued during the next fiscal year to a very large amount. However much we may deprecate it, this will be an imperative necessity which we cannot avoid. However much this may be a departure from sound business and financial principles applicable to times of peace, we must not shrink from the responsibility which is fixed upon us in the execution of this war."—*Ibid.*, p. 2767.

[2] *Statutes at Large*, Vol. XII, p. 592.

[3] Sec. 1. There were likewise similar provisions for deposit and funding.

[4] July 17, 1862.—*Ibid.*, p. 592; *Globe*, Thirty-seventh Congress, 2d Sess., pp. 3402, 3405. The total issue of postage currency, which commenced August 21, 1862, and ended May 27, 1863, was $21,215,635.—KNOX, *op. cit.*, p. 104.

[5] In a silver dollar there were 371.25 grains of fine silver; in two half-dollars, four quarter-dollars, or ten dimes there were only 345.6 grains. At the ratio at which gold was selling in 1862, a silver dollar was worth 104 cents in gold, two half-dollars but 97.—LAUGHLIN, *op. cit.*, Appendix II, F.

This act likewise authorized the use of postage stamps for "payment of all dues of the United States less than $5," and their receipt in exchange for United States notes for such sums.

On January 17, 1863,[1] by a joint resolution, the issue of $100,000,000 more of legal-tender non-interest-bearing notes in denominations not less than $1 was authorized for the purpose of paying the army and navy; and by an act of March 3, 1863,[2] $150,000,000, including the $100,000,000[3] of the joint resolution, similar to those of the first legal-tender act, except as to denomination, were provided for. By this act a substitute for the postage currency was provided,[4] but these notes thus authorized were receivable only for public dues, excepting import duties, to the amount of $5, and were not a tender in private transactions.

By this act, too, a new kind of treasury note was authorized with the legal-tender quality, i. e., $400,000,000 in notes, payable at such time, not exceeding three years from date of issue, as the secretary should find beneficial, bearing interest at a rate not greater than 6 per cent., the interest to be paid in "lawful money" of denominations not less than $10, to be a legal tender, as in the case of United States notes, "for their face value, excluding interest." They were exchangeable, together with accumulated interest, for United States non-interest-bearing notes.

On June 30, 1864,[5] $200,000,000 in interest-bearing[6] notes were authorized, to be a legal tender for their face value, exclusive of interest.[7] On January 28, 1865, this amount

---

[1] *Statutes at Large*, Vol. XII, p. 822.   [2] *Ibid.*, p. 709.   [3] Sec. 3.

[4] To the amount of $50,000,000.—Sec. 4. The total amount of issues and reissues under this and the act of July 17, 1862, was $368,720,074.—KNOX, *op. cit.*, p. 104. These notes were exchangeable, together with accumulated interest, for the non-interest-bearing legal tenders.

[5] *Statutes at Large*, Vol. XIII, p. 218.   [6] At a rate not greater than 7.3 per cent.

[7] And such of them as shall be made payable, principal and interest, at maturity shall be a legal tender to the same extent as United States notes for their face values, excluding interest, etc.

was raised to $400,000,000 by the last act of the war confer-
ring power to issue legal-tender government notes.[1]

A word must be given, also, to a form of notes having
the peculiar quality of being receivable for import duties,
which was authorized by the act of March 3, 1863.[2] By
section 5 of that act, the secretary of the treasury was given
power to receive deposits of gold coin and bullion, for which
certificates in denominations of not less than $20 should be
issued, which should "be received at par in payment for duties
on imports." These certificates were, of course, wholly different from the notes previously described, being evidences of
value received, rather than general promises to pay, given
by the government.

From this statement of the legislation it appears that
$450,000,000[3] of United States legal-tender notes, besides
fractional currency to the amount of $50,000,000, was
authorized during the years of the contest. On January 30,
1864, notes of this character to an amount equal to $449,-
338,902 had been issued.[4] By July 11 they had depreciated
until $100 in notes was worth only $35.09 in gold.[5] Their
use had been understood and declared to be a war measure,
forced by direst necessity. With the cessation of the war
and the lightening of the apparent necessity came movements
looking toward a reduction of the amount of outstanding
notes. A sketch of the legislation looking to this reduction
will not be out of place.

By an act of April 12, 1866,[6] it was provided that during

---

[1] January 28, 1865.—*Ibid.*, p. 425.

[2] *Ibid.*, Vol. XII, p. 709. The use of these was discontinued January 1, 1879, by
executive order.—*United States Treasury Circular* No. 123, p. 11: "Information Respecting United States Bonds, Paper Currency," etc., July 1, 1896.

[3] $50,000,000 being renewed for temporary loans by the act of July 11, 1862, sec. 3.

[4] *United States Treasury Circular* No. 123, p. 10.

[5] Spaulding, *History of the Legal Tender Paper Currency of the Great Rebellion*
(Buffalo, 1869), p. 206; *Report of Monetary Commission*, p. 415.

[6] *Statutes at Large*, Vol. XIV, p. 31.

the next six months United States notes might be retired to
the extent of $10,000,000; after that time not more than
$4,000,000 a month should be withdrawn. This act remained
in force until suspended on February 4, 1868,[1] after the
withdrawal of $44,000,000 of notes.[2]

By an act of January 14, 1875,[3] provision was made for
the resumption of specie payments and the reduction of the
amount of outstanding legal-tender notes; but the process
was again stopped on May 31, 1878, by legislation, which
required that the notes once redeemed should be reissued.[4]

Brief notice only will be given to other forms of notes
which have possessed the power of receivability to a greater
or less extent. The gold certificates authorized by the act
of March 3, 1863, and suspended in 1879, were revived by an
act of July 12, 1882, by which the secretary of the treasury
was " authorized and directed " to receive gold coin and issue
certificates "in denominations of not less than $20 each,
corresponding with the denominations of the United States
notes," which "shall be receivable for customs, taxes, and
all public dues, and when so received, may be reissued."[5]
By the act of February 28, 1878, which "remonetized"
the standard silver dollar,[6] were authorized similar deposits
of silver bullion, and the issue of similar certificates, receivable in like manner with the gold certificates.[7] Lastly, by
an act of July 14, 1890, treasury notes possessing the full

[1] *Statutes at Large*, Vol. XV, p. 34.

[2] *United States Treasury Circular* No. 123, p. 10. In 1873, a large proportion of
these canceled notes were reissued.

[3] *Statutes at Large*, Vol. XVIII, p. 296.

[4] *Ibid.*, Vol. XX, p. 87. Nothing was said of their being legal tender after reissue.
But see the discussion of Juillard *v.* Greenman, below, p. 133.

[5] *Statutes at Large*, Vol. XXII, p. 162, sec. 12.

[6] Above, p. 99; *Statutes at Large*, Vol. XX, p. 25.

[7] Sec. 3. The denomination was to be not lower than $10. "Such certificates
shall be receivable for customs, taxes, and all public dues."

legal-tender quality were again authorized. By that act[1] the secretary of the treasury was directed to purchase each month 4,500,000 ounces of fine silver at the market prices, and pay for it with treasury notes redeemable on demand in coin, which[2] "should be a legal tender in payments of all debts, public and private, except where otherwise expressly stipulated in the contract,[3] and shall be receivable for customs, taxes, and all public dues."[4]

The legislation of February 25, 1862, was distinguished from all measures previously enacted for the purpose of authorizing government notes by the words "shall be lawful money, and a legal tender in all debts, public and private, within the United States." Previous issues had been made receivable in payments to the government and payable to all creditors of the government who would receive them voluntarily at par. With the exception of the single class of revenues, import duties, and the single class of creditors, holders of the public debt, the holders of these notes were to have the legal right of passing them in all transactions to which the government was a party. Members of the army, the navy, the civil service, contractors, were to receive them for their services and goods; and to all collectors of the revenue, with the one exception mentioned, could they be paid. The question at once arose as to the revenues of the states. Did Congress intend to require the officers of the separate commonwealths to receive them? Or give to the citizen the right to use them in settling with his local govern-

[1] *Ibid.*, Vol. XXVI, p. 289, sec. 2.

[2] Note Appendix II, Specie Contracts, below, p. 157.

[3] No greater or less amount of these notes was to be outstanding at any time than the cost of the silver bullion and the standard silver dollars coined from it. The authority for the purchase of silver under this act was revoked November 1, 1893.

[4] *Statutes at Large*, Vol. XXVIII, p. 4. A portion of the act of 1890 was repealed November 1, 1893, when it was declared to be the policy of the United States "to maintain the equal power of every dollar coined or issued by the United States in the market or in the payment of debts."

ment? Did "debts public" include state taxes? The question as to whether the act was intended to include these involuntary obligations to the state preceded any questions of power to do so, and was answered in the negative by the Supreme Court in 1868,[1] so that the question of power to include them did not have to be raised. The intention to exclude these particular obligations was found expressed in the portions of the act in which provision was made for obligations to the federal government, showing that "debts" were to be understood as voluntary obligations, arising out of contract.[2]

But not only was the policy inaugurated by this act with regard to creditors of the government wholly novel; never had the government ventured to include transactions between private individuals in the list of those in which its notes were to pass. As has been seen, coin had been made a legal tender, and Congress had been given express power to pass bankruptcy laws;[3] with these exceptions control over contracts had been held to lie wholly within the realm of state jurisdiction.

The question arose as to the effect of the act on so-called specie contracts,[4] i. e., contracts in terms not simply of money units, but of specific kinds of coin. This question, together with that of the power of Congress in the whole matter, came before the state courts within a short time after the passage of the act,[5] but was brought before the Supreme Court and there settled only in 1868,[6] when again, not the power of Congress, but the application of the act, was limited. It was then decided that such contracts were not within the

---

[1] Lane County v. Oregon, 7 Wallace, 71.

[2] This interpretation was put upon the act in 1862 by Justice Field, then chief justice of the supreme court of California, 20 Cal. 350.

[3] *Constitution of the United States*, I, 8, 4.

[4] See Appendix II for note on specie contracts; below, p. 157.

[5] See Appendix I for note on decisions of state courts; below, p. 156.

[6] Bronson v. Rodes, 7 Wallace, 229.

meaning of the act,[1] and contracts for coin were treated as contracts for bullion, which might be enforced in the terms of the contract, the money terms being taken as descriptive of weight and fineness simply.[2]

By these two important decisions the application of the act of February 25, 1862, had been successively limited in application. The question of constitutional power within its scope had not, however, been determined by the final tribunal. A large majority of the commonwealth courts had upheld it[3] within the narrow limits within which the Supreme Court decisions had confined its operations, as well as sustained its application to a larger range of transactions. A decision adverse to the validity of the act arrived at by the Kentucky court of appeals[4] had brought the question before the Supreme Court of the United States, and, after argument and re-argument, the court finally handed down its opinion in February of 1870, in a decision adverse to the power claimed by Congress.[5]

In arriving at this conclusion, the distinction was drawn between contracts entered into before the passage of the act and those of a subsequent date, and the question arose in this case as to the application of the act to the former of these

---

[1] It was argued that, since import duties were to be paid in coin, coin contracts must have been excluded from legislation, which would otherwise have rendered them impossible.

[2] The judgment being entered in the kind of dollars named in the contract, interest would be required in the same form. " Such a contract is in legal import nothing else than an agreement to deliver a certain weight of standard gold, to be ascertained by the count of coins, each of which is certified to contain a definite proportion of the weight. It is not distinguishable *in principle* from a contract to deliver an equal weight of bullion of equal fineness " (p. 250). There is great force in the reasoning adduced in the dissenting opinion of Justice Miller, that all contracts in terms of dollars should be treated alike, since prior to the act under consideration the legal import was the same. See, also, Butler *v.* Horwitz, 7 Wallace, 268, and Trebilcock *v.* Wilson, 12 Wallace, 687.

[3] See Appendix I, p. 156.   [4] Griswold *v.* Hepburn, 2 Duval (Ky.), 26.

[5] This question was first argued before the Supreme Court at the December term, 1867; it was reargued in December, 1868. The opinion was handed down in February, 1870.—Hepburn *v.* Griswold, 8 Wallace, p. 603.

two classes. The court held that the clear intent of the act was manifested to include prior contracts, and, so far, was an excess of power under the constitution, and therefore void.

Interest in this decision is quickened by the fact that the chief justice who handed down the opinion of the court was identical with the secretary of the treasury who permitted, if he did not urge, the measure. A comparison of the firm and unwavering argument of the judge is in marked contrast with the somewhat uncertain statement of the secretary.[1] It gains an added interest by reason of its futility as an effort to set right some of the unfortunate effects of the policy of the government in monetary matters. It was a brave, if futile, effort to correct as judge blunders made as executive.

The argument of the majority[2] may be briefly stated as follows: Every contract for money units made before the passage of the act was, in legal import, a contract for coin. These notes were liable to depreciation, and in proportion to their depreciation their enforced receipt was an impairment of the contract and contrary to justice and equity, and could be accomplished only if the power was plain. It was not claimed that the power was expressly granted, and so the definition of the implied powers given in McCulloch v. Maryland was drawn upon: "Appropriate, plainly adapted to the end sought; not prohibited, but con-

[1] "The provision making the United States notes a legal tender has doubtless been well considered by the committee, and their conclusion needs no support from any observation of mine. I think it my duty, however, to say that in respect to this provision my reflections have conducted me to the same conclusion they have reached."—Chase's letter, January 29, 1862, quoted by SPAULDING, *op. cit.*, p. 45; above, p. 116.

[2] The majority consisted of Chief Justice Chase and Justices Nelson, Clifford, Grier, and Field. Justices Miller, Swayne, and Davis dissented. Justice Grier was forced by ill-health to resign between the date on which the decision was ordered and that on which it was handed down. Nelson, Grier, and Clifford were already on the bench when Lincoln became president. Field, Chase, Swayne, Miller, and Davis were his appointees.—HART, *Life of Salmon Portland Chase*, American States-man Series, p. 325.

sistent with the letter and spirit of the constitution." The court held that the power to bestow the legal-tender quality upon notes was not incident to the coinage power, nor identical with the power to issue notes. To sustain this contention, reference was made to the power to issue notes possessed by the Continental Congress, which had never claimed the power to make those notes a legal tender. The power was declared to be no more incident to the power to carry on war than to any other power involving the expenditure of money. It was asserted that the legal-tender quality had not as a matter of fact affected the value of the notes, as was shown by the circulation of notes not possessing that quality; and, since it impaired the obligation of contracts, it was contrary to the spirit of the constitution, as manifested in the prohibition laid on the states[1] and in that contained in the fifth amendment.[2]

It is interesting to note that the minority did not deny that the effect of the act was to impair the obligation of contracts, which they held, not being prohibited to Congress, was within its competence. They maintained that this power to bestow the legal-tender quality upon notes was clearly incident to the power to borrow money, to raise and support armies, etc.; and disputed the truth of the history of the legal-tender notes as stated in the majority opinion.

The failure of the minority to advance the argument that the obligation of the contract was an obligation to pay in what was lawful money at the time of payment, and so was not impaired, is striking, because this had been advanced with great force in the state courts,[3] and was afterwards advanced and approved by the majority in overruling the

[1] I, 10, 1.

[2] "Nor shall any person be deprived of life, liberty, or property without due process of law."

[3] See Legal Tender Cases, 52 Pa. St., 9; Griswold v. Hepburn, 2 Duval (Ky.), 26 (dissenting opinion).

decision now being considered.[1] At this time not even
those who sustained the power were willing to base it, even
indirectly, on the ancient doctrine of prerogative.

The act was thus held to be void as to contracts entered
into before the date of its passage. The decision, however,
failed to receive general acquiescence. The material and
corporate interests involved were, of course, enormous;[2] there
was, too, a certain patriotic sentiment for the paper money
with which the war had been fought out; the administration,[3] Congress, and popular prejudice, all were opposed to
the court; and its position was one peculiarly adapted
to obtaining a reconsideration. The court had consisted,
when the decision in Hepburn v. Griswold had been
reached, of eight members, a chief justice and seven associate justices. Before the opinion was handed down Justice
Grier had been forced to resign.[4] In 1866[5] an act had gone
into effect providing that no vacancies in the Supreme bench
should be filled until the number of associate justices was
reduced to six. This was repealed in 1869,[6] and the number of justices increased to nine. To the two vacancies thus
created Justice Strong and Justice Bradley were appointed.
Justice Strong had had opportunity on the bench of Pennsylvania to express his views on this question,[7] so that his
position in support of the act was well known. Of Justice
Bradley it is said that all that was known of his views was

---

[1] Legal Tender Cases, 12 Wallace, 457.

[2] "At that time gold stood at about 120; so that, if the decision [Hepburn v.
Griswold] held, all debts and obligations would speedily represent one and one-
fifth times their value as here expressed in greenbacks. This was the weak point
for the court, for it set against it the powerful influence of many corporations
. . . . with maturing *ante bellum* obligation."—HART, *op. cit.*, p. 397. On this point
see an article on "Constitutional Interpretation" by Professor Bascom, *Yale Review*,
Vol. X, p. 350. Also SHUCKERS, *op. cit.*, p. 261.

[3] HART, *op. cit.*, chap. X.   [4] 7 Wallace, p. VII.

[5] July 23, *Statutes at Large*, Vol. XIV, p. 209. This act is said to have been the
result of spite against President Johnson.

[6] April 10, *ibid.*, Vol. XVI, p. 44.   [7] 52 Pa. St., 9.

the fact that as counselor for a corporation he had advised the payment of their obligations in gold as a matter of honor.[1] In case of a reconsideration, the decisive vote would of course be cast by him.

On motion of the attorney general a reconsideration of the legal-tender question was ordered immediately upon the completion of the court[2] in two cases, which were afterward dismissed. Not until the following year was Hepburn v. Griswold formally overruled as to prior contracts; but the country had understood from the previous action of the court that the question was entirely open, and the act was then held to apply to contracts entered into both before and after its passage.[3]

This reversal of a decision so recently announced by so slight a change of relative numbers in the majority and minority of the court, with the change of personnel so prominent a factor in the situation, constitutes a unique feature in the history of the American Supreme Court. All considerations of judicial dignity, of regard for precedent, of desire for the stability of the law, would have led to acquiescence in the decision, or at least such a decent delay in its reconsideration as would have allowed new arguments to be advanced, new elements in the general condition of affairs to appear;[4] or, it might have been allowed to stand as to prior con-

[1] See the letter of Senator Hoar to E. J. James, *American Economic Association*, Vol. III, p. 50. It is unnecessary to state and refute the charges of personal corruption of the justices freely made at the time. Even if the lowest view of the situation is taken, it is wholly unnecessary to adduce motives of personal corruption in the then existing state of public sentiment. Still, a statement of the history of the court would be incomplete without reference to them. A most interesting paper describing the methods of coming to a decision has just been published by Justice Bradley's heirs. —See Appendix III, p. 160.

[2] Justice Bradley was sworn in March 23, 1871, and the attorney general moved a reconsideration on March 25.

[3] Legal Tender Cases, 12 Wallace, 457.

[4] For the other side of the argument, *i. e.*, for reasons for immediate reconsideration, see the article on "Constitutional Interpretation" by Professor Bascom, *loc. cit.*, Vol. X, p. 350.

tracts, and the application of the act to subsequent contracts might have been sustained. Those considerations of a political and material character which demanded its reconsideration,[1] however, prevailed. Whether the result of the reconsideration be accepted as good law or not, the fact of such a change under such circumstances must be universally regarded as a deplorable incident in the history of the United States judiciary.

In this decision,[2] as in the former arguments, appeal was had to considerations of public policy. The idea of resulting powers—that is, such as were not expressly conferred by the constitution, but were incident to a group of those so bestowed—was developed, and the power to bestow the legal-tender quality upon bills of the government was classed among such powers. The argument that the obligation of contracts had not been impaired, because that obligation consisted in the duty to pay such money as was lawful at the time of payment, that is, the principle of the Case of Mixt Monies, which had been on the former occasion rejected by the minority, was now advanced; but, as before, it was maintained that, even if this was not the law, Congress had the power to impair such obligations.

The distinction between contracts entered into before and after the date of the passage of the act was denied, and the act was held to apply to both classes and to be a legitimate exercise of power. Stress was laid upon the exigency existing at the time, and upon the necessity of full power over sword and purse; and, finally, the power was held to exist as a war power.[3]

Justice Field's contribution to the argument of the

[1] Legal Tender Cases, 12 Wallace, 457.

[2] Justice Strong delivered the opinion of the court, Justice Bradley giving a concurring opinion, while the dissenting justices each gave his opinion at length.

[3] Justice Bradley logically refused to limit the existence of the power to the duration of an exigency arising out of war, but declared that the question of the existence of that exigency was a legislative question, as had been argued by the counsel against the act.

minority[1] is a masterly analysis of the true nature of the contract of borrowing, which should not be omitted:

The terms "power to borrow money" . . . . have not one meaning when used by individuals and another when granted to corporations, and still a different one when possessed by Congress. They mean only a power to contract for a loan of money upon consideration to be agreed between the parties. The amount of the loan, the time of payment, the interest it shall bear, and the form in which the obligation shall be expressed are simply matters of arrangement between the parties. As to the loan and security for its repayment, the borrower may of course pledge such property as revenues, and annex to his promises such privileges, as he may possess. His stipulations in this respect are necessarily limited to his own property rights and privileges, and cannot extend to those of other persons.

According to the decision, then, the power exercised by Congress in authorizing the issue of legal-tender notes was a legitimate power in time of war, and such notes could be employed to cancel obligations growing out of contracts entered into both before and after the passage of that act, provided that such obligations assumed the form neither of involuntary obligations to commonwealth governments nor of contracts in terms of specific forms of coins.

The act of May 31, 1878,[2] brought up the question whether or not it was a power to be exercised in time of peace. That act said nothing, in declaring that the legal-tender notes, after being canceled, should be reissued, as to whether or not they should be reissued as legal tender; but that quality was claimed for them. The question came before the Supreme Court in 1883,[3] and by a vote almost unanimous (8 to 1) it was decided that Congress had the power in time of peace to bestow this quality on the issues of the government. The power was declared by the court

---

[1] Formerly the majority.

[2] *Statutes at Large*, Vol. XX, p. 87; above, p. 124.

[3] Juillard v. Greenman, 110 U. S., 421.

to be incident to that of borrowing, "the power to raise money for the public use on a pledge of the public credit" including the power "to issue, in return for the money borrowed, the obligation of the United States in any appropriate form of stock, bonds, bills, or notes . . . . adapted to circulation from hand to hand in the ordinary transactions of business." The general power of Congress over the currency of the country is then adduced. Congress has the power, argues the court, to incorporate national banks, with the capacity for their own profit as well as for the use of the government in its money transactions of issuing bills which under ordinary circumstances pass from hand to hand as money at their nominal value, and which, when so current, the law has always recognized as a good tender in payment of money debts, unless specifically objected to at the time of the tender.[1] The constitutional authority of Congress to provide a currency for the whole country, in the form either of a coin circulation or by the emission of bills of credit, is now fully established. These powers over the currency, to coin, to emit bills, and to make anything other than gold and silver a legal tender, are prohibited to the states. From this it follows that Congress has the power to issue the obligations of the United States in such form, and to impress upon them such qualities as currency as accord with the use of sovereign governments. And, as a third argument, resort is had to the doctrine of sovereignty:

The power as incident to the power of borrowing money and issuing bills or notes of the government for money borrowed, of impressing upon those bills or notes the quality of being a legal tender for the payment of private debts, was a power universally understood to belong to sovereignty in Europe and America at the time of framing and adopting the constitution of the United States.[2]

[1] In this extraordinary statement the court ignores the fact that when a form of money is a tender the creditor cannot object to receiving it.

[2] Juillard v. Greenman, 110 U. S., 447.

Under the power to borrow money on the credit of the United States and to issue circulating notes for the money borrowed, its [Congress's] power to define the quality and force of those notes as currency is as broad as the like power over the metallic currency under the power to coin money and to regulate the value thereof.

Congress, as the legislature of a sovereign nation, being expressly empowered by the constitution to lay and collect taxes, to pay the debts, and provide for the common defense and general welfare of the United States, and to "borrow money on the credit of the United States," and "to coin money and regulate the value thereof, and of foreign coin," and being clearly authorized as incidental to the exercise of those great powers to emit bills of credit, to charter national banks, and to provide a national currency for the whole people in the form of coin, treasury notes, and national bank bills, and the power to make the notes of the government a legal tender in payment of private debts being one of the powers belonging to sovereignty in other civilized nations, and not expressly withheld from Congress by the constitution, we are irresistibly impelled to the conclusion that the impressing upon the treasury notes of the United States the quality of being a legal tender in payment of private debts is an appropriate means, conducive and plainly adapted to the execution of the undoubted power of Congress, consistent with the letter and spirit of the constitution, and therefore, within the meaning of that instrument, "necessary and proper for carrying into execution the powers vested by this constitution in the government of the United States."

Of the dissenting opinion by Justice Field, two important points should be noticed. Objection is raised by him to "the rule of construction adopted by the court to reach its conclusions, a rule which, fully carried out, would change the whole nature of our constitution and break down the barriers which separate a government of limited from one of unlimited powers." The second is the denial of the argument from sovereignty:

Of what purpose, in the light of the tenth amendment, is it, then, to refer to the exercise of the power by the absolute or the limited government of Europe or by the states previous to the constitution?

Congress can exercise no power by virtue of any supposed inherent sovereignty in the general government. Indeed, it may be doubted whether the power can be correctly said to appertain to sovereignty in any proper sense as an attribute of an independent political community. The power to commit violence, perpetrate injustice, take private property by force without compensation to the owner, and compel the receipt of promise to pay in place of money, may be exercised, as it often has been, by irresponsible authority, but it cannot be considered as belonging to a government founded upon law.[1]

This objection from this minority of one gains force when it is realized that for an analogous act on the part of the English government, from which American ideas of sovereign power are drawn, we should have to go back to the reign of Henry VIII.

It is evident, however, that the bases for a decision either favorable or adverse to the exercise of this power are large considerations of public policy, of constitutional interpretations, of judicial policy, rather than strictly legal considerations. The substratum of law, in the principle of the Case of Mixt Monies, was at first distinctly, if not expressly, rejected in the admission that such legislation, applied to pre-existing agreements, did impair the obligation of contracts. And while men differ on these questions of public policy[2] and constitutional interpretation, they will disagree as to the legal-tender decisions; but there has been a general acquiescence in them and there is apparently no prospect of their being reopened. The whole question has become one within the discretion, since within the power, of Congress.

From this inquiry into the extent to which the quality of being *current*, using that word in the older sense of the

[1] Juillard *v.* Greenman, 110 U. S., p. 466.

[2] In support of the decisions, see particularly Professor THAYER, "Legal Tender," *Harvard Law Review*, Vol. I, p. 70; HARE, *Constitutional Law of the United States*, chap. 57. As opposed may be cited BANCROFT, *The Constitution Wounded in the House of its Guardians*, and TUCKER, *Constitution of the United States*, secs. 509, 510.

English proclamation, has been bestowed upon government issues, the following results emerge : (1) On no notes issued during the period prior to 1862 was the quality of being a tender in private transactions bestowed. (2) On all the notes issued during that period was bestowed the quality of being receivable for all public dues. (3) Upon the notes authorized in 1890, and upon them alone, was bestowed the quality of being both a tender in private transactions and receivable in all payments to the government. (4) The power to bestow the quality of being a tender in private transactions has been adjudged an incident to sovereign powers vested in Congress similar to the ancient prerogative money power of the English Crown.

CHAPTER XI

NOTES OF BANKS ORGANIZED UNDER FEDERAL AND STATE AUTHORITY

The First and Second Banks of the United States — The National Banking System — State-Bank Notes — The Webster Resolutions, 1816—The Treasury Circular, 1836.

THE notes of the United States banks and of the banks chartered by the separate states have never had the full legal-tender quality bestowed upon them; yet both classes of notes have been given a limited currency, and have been the occasion of such interesting federal action as to bring them under the definition laid down[1] and to make a discussion of them here appropriate. The notes of institutions chartered under federal authority will first be considered.

The creation of a national bank formed an important item in the plans of Hamilton for the creation and establishment of the public credit, and in accordance with the suggestions made by him in his "Report on a National Bank," presented to Congress on December 6, 1790,[2] a bill was introduced in the House of Representatives having for its object the creation of such an institution, and became a law February 25, 1792.[3] By section 10 of this act the bills and

---

[1] Above, p. 3.

[2] In answer to a resolution calling on him for further suggestions for the support of the public credit.—*Annals of Congress*, Vol. I, p. 1722; also Appendix, p. 2031. The discussion provoked by this bill will be found below, Appendix IV, p. 169.

[3] The bank was chartered for twenty years; there were to be twenty-five directors, for whom only stockholders who were resident citizens of the United States could vote; no foreigner could be a director; a fourth of the directors were elected each year. Reports were to be made to the secretary of the treasury at his request, not oftener than weekly, and he could inspect the books, except private accounts. Real property could be held only for the use of the bank or for foreclosure. Loans of over $100,000 could be made to the United States only with the consent of Congress; $50,000 was the limit of loans to the United States, and none could be made to foreign potentates. No notes under $10 were to be issued.—*Statutes at Large*, Vol. I, p. 191.

notes of the corporation which were made payable, or which
had become payable, on demand in gold or silver coin were
made receivable in all payments to the United States, and
were so far a lawful tender.[1] This provision was repealed
March 19, 1812,[2] the existence of the bank having terminated by the conditions of the charter on February 25 of
that year. A similar provision[3] was inserted in the charter
of the Second Bank of the United States, authorized April
10, 1816,[4] and repealed June 15, 1836,[5] after the termination of that institution's existence.[6]

During the period, then, from 1792 (February 25) to
1812 (March 19), and from 1816 (April 10) until 1836 (June
15), the notes of the Bank of the United States were a legal
tender in all payments to the United States.

After a period of twenty-five years a project for the
organization, not of a bank, but of a system of banks, was
again brought forward, this time under the pressure of the
Civil War. The plan for such a system was outlined by Secretary Chase in his report of December, 1861,[7] and again
urged by him in December, 1862,[8] and on January 19, 1863,[9]
was made the subject of a special message to Congress.
In accordance with these suggestions a bill "to provide a
national currency secured by a pledge of United States
stocks, and to provide for the circulation and redemption of
the same," was introduced into the House of Representatives

[1] "That the bills or notes of the said corporation originally made payable, or
which shall have become payable, on demand in gold and silver coin, shall be
receivable in all payments to the United States."

[2] *Ibid.*, Vol. II, p. 695.

[3] Identical in terms, except for the proviso, " unless otherwise directed by act of
Congress."

[4] *Ibid.*, Vol. III, p. 266, sec. 14.   [5] *Ibid.*, Vol. V, p. 48.

[6] April 10, 1836, by the terms of its charter.—See *Debates of Congress* 1831-32,
Appendix, p. 73; SUMNER, *History of Banking in the United States*, p. 210.

[7] *Globe*, Thirty-seventh Congress, 2d Sess., Appendix, p. 25.

[8] *Ibid.*, 3d Sess., Appendix, p. 25.   [9] *Ibid.*, p. 881.

on July 11, 1862,[1] into the Senate January 26, 1863,[2] and
became a law February 25, 1863.[3] This law proved unsatis-
factory, however, and was repealed and superseded by an act
of similar title which became a law June 3, 1864.[4]

The system as created in 1863 and modified in 1864 consisted of associations organized for the period of twenty
years,[5] with a minimum capital of $50,000;[6] the smallest
deposit for circulation being $30,000.[7] On such deposit of
United States notes an amount equal to ninety cents on the
dollar of market value, not exceeding par, was to be furnished
in circulating notes by an officer of the Treasury Department.[8]
The lowest denomination of these notes was to be one dollar
until after resumption of specie payments, and then $5.[9] The
amount of notes for circulation was limited to $300,000,000.[9]
The banks in the sixteen leading cities were required to maintain a reserve of *lawful money* equal to 25 per cent. of their
circulation and deposits; all others were to keep 15 per
cent.[10] The amount of indebtedness was limited to the amount
of capital paid in.[11]

Quarterly reports were to be published in the newspapers.[12] A tax of 1 per cent. was laid on the average
amount of circulation, of one-half of 1 per cent. on the
deposits, and the same on the capital stock not invested in
United States bonds; and a state tax on the shares not
greater than the rate at which other moneyed capital was

---

[1] *Globe*, Thirty-seventh Congress, 2d Sess., p. 3258.   [2] *Ibid.*, 3d Sess., p. 505.

[3] *Statutes at large*, Vol. XII, p. 665.   [4] *Ibid.*, Vol. XIII, p. 99.

[5] Extended twenty years by act of July 12, 1882.—*Ibid.*, Vol. XXII, p. 162.

[6] $50,000 in places of not over 6,000 population; $200,000 in places of over 50,000
population; $100,000 for places between those limits.—Act of 1864, sec. 7. Of this one-
half had to be paid in before beginning operations.—Sec. 14.

[7] Or one-third of capital stock paid in.—Sec. 15.

[8] Sec. 21. This was altered March 3, 1865, to a smaller proportion, so that a bank
with more than $3,000,000 capital could have only 60 per cent.—*Ibid.*, Vol. XIII, p.
498.

[9] Sec. 22.   [10] Sec. 31.

[11] Sec. 36.   [12] Sec. 34.—See *ibid.*, Vol. XV, p. 326.

taxed [1] was allowed to be imposed by the state in which
the shares were located.

The notes of the banks so organized were made receivable at par in all parts of the United States, in payment of
taxes, excises, public lands, and all other dues to the United
States, except for duties on imports, and for all salaries and
other debts and demands owing by the United States to individuals, corporations, and associations within the United
States, except interest on the public debt and in redemption
of the national currency. [2] The notes were also to be taken
at par by all the banking associations formed under the act. [3]

So much for the notes of banks authorized by federal
authority. As to the notes of institutions existing under
charters granted by the respective commonwealths, it may be
remarked that the constitution of the United States was
silent on the subject of the power of the states to grant charters of incorporation to banking institutions; but at the time
of its adoption and in the years immediately following the
states were exercising this power freely. [4] There was no question or controversy as to the power of the states in this direction until, in the second and the early part of the third decade
of the nineteenth century, two influences led to their power
being questioned. One of these influences was the effort
put forth by some of the states to evade by means of so-called

[1] Sec. 41.

[2] Sec. 23: "and the same shall be received *at par* in all parts of the United
States in payment of taxes, excises, public lands and all other dues to the United
States, except for duties on imports, and also for all salaries and other debts and
demands owing by the United States to individuals, corporations, and associations
within the United States, except interest on the public debt and in redemption of
the national currency."

[3] Sec. 32: "Every association formed or existing under the provisions of this
act shall take and receive at par for any liability to the said association any and all
notes or bills issued by any association existing under and by virtue of this act."

[4] The Bank of Massachusetts was chartered February 7, 1784; that of Maryland,
1790; of Providence, 1791; of Albany, Boston, Alexandria, and Richmond, 1792; and
the Bank of South Carolina, unchartered, began operation that same year.—Sumner,
History of Banking in the United States, p. 19.

"banking institutions" the prohibition of the constitution against their issuing bills of credit ; the other was the alignment of those in favor of state banks in opposition to those who favored federal banks, and the denial by the latter of the legitimacy of issues of such organizations as conflicted with the federal institutions.

The efforts on the part of the states to avoid the prohibition against bills of credit assumed two forms. The first was that selected by the state of Missouri when, in 1821, its legislature enacted a law providing for the issue of loan certificates signed by state officers to the amount of $200,000, in denominations of from fifty cents to $10, which should be receivable for public dues and by public creditors, these certificates to be secured by the income from salt springs belonging to the state, and by the faith of the state, which was pledged for their repayment. The legitimacy of this issue came before the Supreme Court in 1830,[1] and these loan certificates were decided to be " bills of credit issued by the state" of Missouri, and so prohibited. The court then defined the term "bills of credit," as used in the constitution, as "paper intended to circulate through the community for its ordinary purposes as money, which paper is redeemable at a future day," or "a paper medium intended to circulate between individuals or between government and individuals, for the ordinary purposes of society."

Kentucky had adopted a different method of accomplishing this evasion, and had chartered a so-called "Bank of the Commonwealth of Kentucky."[2] Of this bank the stock was owned by the state, the officers were elected annually by the legislature, and their salaries were paid by the state. This organization was to issue $2,000,000[3] worth of notes, which were to be apportioned among the counties in pro-

[1] Craig v. The State of Missouri, 4 Peters, 410.   [2] November 29, 1820.
[3] Increased the next month to $3,000,000.

portion to the taxable property, on mortgage securities, and, as it was naïvely said, to loan to such as needed the notes "for paying his or her just and honest debts." Its capital was to consist of all money paid in for land warrants for certain public lands, of produce of stock owned by the state in the Bank of Kentucky, and unexpected balances in the treasury at the end of each year.[1] Profits went to the state, and the notes were receivable for public dues and by public creditors.

The legality of this corporation and its notes came first before the Supreme Court in 1834,[2] but was decided only in 1837, because of the change in the personnel of the bench and its being incomplete[3] during that period.

In the argument of this case, the definitions laid down in Craig v. Missouri were quoted and applied; it was also maintained that the state could not do indirectly what it could not do directly; but the court rejected the definition previously given and substituted for it a much narrower one, viz.: "to constitute a bill of credit, within the constitution, it must be issued by the state, on the faith of the state, and be designed to circulate as money. It must be a paper which circulates on the credit of the state and is so received and used in the ordinary business of life. Those who issue must have power to bind the state." From this definition notes issued by banks, by individuals, by municipal corporations, are all excluded; and the argument that the state can-

---

[1] Substantially the only capital the bank ever had was $7,000 appropriated by the legislature to buy books, paper, and slates.

[2] A suit on a note drawn in 1830, the defense being "no consideration" because the consideration had consisted of notes of that bank.—John Briscoe *et al. v.* The President and Directors of the Bank of the Commonwealth of Kentucky, 11 Peters, 257.

[3] In 1834 two judges were absent; of the five who heard the argument, three thought the notes were within the prohibition. The court was not complete until March, 1836, and the decision was rendered in January, 1837. Although the Kentucky court of appeals had sustained the legitimacy of the bank, one of the Kentucky circuit courts in 1834 had decided against it in the case of Bank v. Mayes.—Sumner, *History of Banking in the United States*, p. 142.

not do indirectly what it cannot do directly was rejected on the ground that to admit its validity would be to deny the legitimacy of state banks, and their legality could not be questioned.

The hostility to state banks felt by those who favored the federal institutions was expressed by Webster when speaking of the renewal of the charter of the Second Bank of the United States.[1] He claimed for the federal government, on the ground of its control over the coinage, complete and exclusive control over the currency of the country, and suggested the illegality of state banks, admitting, however, that up to that time there had been no controversy on the question.[2]

[1] May 25 and 28, 1832.

[2] *Webster's Works*, Vol. III, p. 395: "We all know, sir, that the establishment of a sound and uniform currency was one of the great ends contemplated in the adoption of the present constitution. . . . . It cannot well be questioned that it was intended by that constitution to submit the whole subject of the currency of the country, all that regards the actual medium of payment and exchange, whatever that should be, to the control and legislation of Congress. . . . . The exclusive power of regulating the metallic currency of the country would seem necessarily to imply, or more properly to include as a part of itself, a power to decide how far that currency should be exclusive, how far any substitute should interfere with it, and what that substitute shall be. The generality and extent of the power granted to Congress, and the clear and well-defined prohibition on the states, leave little doubt of the intent to reserve the whole subject of currency from local legislation and to confer it on the general government. Yet . . . . . the currency of the country is now to a great extent practically and effectually under the control of the several state governments . . . . , or rather . . . . of the banking institutions created by the states. A hundred state institutions claim the right of driving coin out of circulation by the introduction of their own paper, and then of depreciating and degrading that paper by refusing to redeem it."

He admitted that there had up to this time been no controversy as to the constitutionality of the power exercised by the states in creating banking corporations, and hoped that none would arise; but on May 28th, speaking in opposition to amendments to the proposed bank charter introduced by an advocate of the local banks, he said (Vol. III, p. 413): "Let me ask whether Congress, if it had not the power of coining money and of regulating the value of foreign coins, could create a bank with the power to circulate bills? For one, I think that it would be difficult to make that out. Where, then, do the states, to whom all control over the metallic currency is altogether prohibited, get the power? It is true that in other countries private banks having no legal authority over the coins issue notes for circulation, but this they do always with the consent of the government, express or implied, and government restrains or regulates all their operations at its pleasure. . . . . I confess, Mr. President, that the more I reflect on the subject the more clearly does my mind approach the conclusion that the creation of state banks for the purpose and

The conflict between the federal bank and the state banks brought forth Webster's arguments against the issues of state banks. In the same way the situation of the Civil War, the increased issues of the state banks due to the absence of restraint after the suspension of specie payments, the use of the legal-tender notes in their reserves and as a basis for extended circulation,[1] and the exigencies of Secretary Chase's plan for a national banking system, caused another attack on the state banks in the form of proposals to tax their issues. In December, 1861, in advocating the duty of the government to furnish a national currency, Secretary Chase laid down the proposition that Congress, under its constitutional power to lay taxes, to regulate commerce, and regulate the issue of coin, possessed ample authority to control the credit circulation of the country.[2] In execution of a part of his plan the system of national banks was created, but it failed to accomplish the end desired, as few state banks reorganized under the act of February 25, 1863. In 1864 the secretary,

with the power of circulating paper is not consistent with the grants and prohibitions of the constitution."

These words are referred to approvingly by STORY in his *Commentaries*, secs. 1358-70. But it must be borne in mind that Webster is speaking as advocate for the national bank.—See KNOX, *History of Banking, etc.*, p. 22; also *Federalist*, No. 44.

Briscoe *v.* Bank of the Commonwealth of Kentucky (1837) decided that the power belonged to the states, even when all the stock and all the profits belonged to the state.

[1] HART, *op. cit.*, p. 275, speaks of 5,000 kinds of notes in circulation. See SHERMAN's speech in Senate February 10, 1863, *Globe*, Thirty-seventh Congress, 3d Sess., p. 841.

[2] In his report, July 4, 1861, the secretary proposed a tax on "distilled liquors, bank notes, carriages, and similar descriptions of property."—*Ibid.*, 1st Sess., Appendix, p. 4. There had been similar taxes for revenue in 1797 (*Statutes at Large*, Vol. I, p. 527), and from 1813 to 1817.—SUMNER, *History of Banking, etc.*, p. 33; BENTON, *Thirty Years' View* (N. Y., 1886), Vol. II, p. 8. Benton had proposed a tax in 1840 for disciplinary purposes, but the Senate refused to consider it, on the ground of lack of power.—*Globe*, Twenty-sixth Congress, 2d Sess., p. 54. In his report, December 9, 1861, Secretary Chase took the ground that "it is too clear to be reasonably disputed that Congress, under its constitutional powers to lay taxes, to regulate commerce, and to regulate the value of coin, possesses ample authority to control the credit circulation which enters so largely into the transactions of commerce and effects in so many ways the value of coin. In the opinion of the secretary, the time has arrived when Congress should exercise this authority."—*Ibid.*, Thirty-seventh Congress, 2d Sess., Appendix, p. 25.

therefore, advocated the imposition of a prohibitory tax on state banks.[1]

The policy of control by taxation had been inaugurated by the passage of an act, March 3, 1863,[2] imposing a tax of 10 per cent. on all fractional notes issued either by state banks or those organized under the federal law. This was continued by an act of March 3, 1865,[3] imposing a similar tax (10 per cent.) on the amount of notes of state banks paid out by any banking organization after July 1 of the following year.[4] The result of this prohibitory tax was, of course, the disappearance of state-bank issues and of the problems arising out of their use.

The question arises as to what recognition was given to these notes by federal authority.

By the "Act to Regulate the Collection of the Duties imposed by Law," of July 31, 1789, it had been provided that

[1] Secretary Fessenden had assumed the duties of secretary of the treasury July 5, 1864.— Report of Secretary of Treasury, *Globe*, Thirty-eighth Congress, 2d Sess., p. 29.

[2] *Statutes at Large*, Vol. XII, p. 709. Such notes had been prohibited the previous July 14.—*Ibid.*, p. 592.

[3] "That every national banking association, state bank, or state banking association shall pay a tax of ten per centum on the amount of notes of any state bank or state banking association paid out by them after July 1, 1866."—*Ibid.*, Vol. XIII, p. 484, sec. 6. Enlarged to include notes of "persons . . . . intended for circulation," July 13, 1866.—*Ibid.*, Vol. XIV, p. 146. And "of any town, city, or municipal corporation," March 26, 1867.— *Ibid.*, Vol. XV, p. 6.

[4] The question of the constitutionality of this act, on the ground that it was a tax on a franchise granted by a state which Congress "on any principle exempting the reserved powers of the states from impairment by taxation must be held to have no authority to lay and collect," came before the Supreme Court and was decided in 1869. The act was upheld on two grounds: (1) the issue of notes, being profitable contracts made by the corporation issuing them, could be made contributive to the public revenue, the rate being a legislative and not a judicial question; (2) that Congress, under the coinage power, expressly conferred, and its power to emit bills of credit, long acquiesced in, could take such steps as seemed necessary to fit its coin and its bills to serve as currency.— Veazie Bank *v.* Fenno, 8 Wallace, 533. Chief Justice Chase handed down the opinion in this case. Since the decision of that case the question has not been widely discussed, although the Democratic platforms of 1892, 1896, and 1900 have either expressly or by implication advocated the repeal of the law.—See *World Almanac*, 1893, p. 88. "We recommend that the prohibitory ten per cent. tax on state-bank issues be repealed."—*Annual Cyclopedia*, 1896, p. 763; *ibid.*, 1900, p. 717.

such duties and fees should be collected in gold and silver coin only.[1] In 1797, when the public lands were being offered for sale, it was agreed that evidences of the public debt might be received in payment.[2]

According to express legislation, then, specie, the evidences of the public debt, and the notes of the Bank of the United States[3] were the only media recognized in the collection of the obligations of the federal government.

During the lifetime of the First Bank of the United States, its notes supplied a large part of the circulating medium. They were received everywhere without question or doubt of their redemption, and through its habit of returning the notes of local banks for redemption it served as a check and regulator of their issues.[4] The expiration of the charter and the refusal of Congress to renew it altered the condition of affairs. To replace one bank with a capital of $10,000,000, one hundred and twenty banks with a capital of $30,000,000 were created.[5] The method of organization and management of these institutions was such as to arouse distrust. The exigencies of war and the exportation of specie incident to winding up the affairs of the federal bank brought about a suspension of specie payments at the end of August, 1814.[6]

Even during the existence of the United States Bank the local banks had been used by the federal government as depositories,[7] and after its expiration the notes of banks in ports of entry were received by the treasury.[8] Because of

---

[1] *Statutes at Large*, Vol. I, p. 45, sec. 30. As there was yet no money of the United States, foreign coins at specified rates were named as the medium.

[2] *Ibid.*, p. 507. See, also, Vol. II, p. 74.

[3] See above, p. 139.

[4] BOLLES, *Financial History of the United States*, Vol. II, p. 261.

[5] SUMNER, *History of Banking in the United States*, p. 64.

[6] BOLLES, *op. cit.*, Vol. II, p. 153.

[7] SUMNER, *op. cit.*, p. 33; Gallatin's *Writings*, Vol. I, p. 102.

[8] *Annals*, Fourteenth Cong., 1st Sess., p. 1230.

this, a great advantage accrued to those merchants who imported goods at ports of entry where the currency was most depreciated. The secretary of the treasury saw no other way out of the difficulty than to ask Congress to strengthen his position by designating specie or its equivalent as the only currency which might be accepted by the treasury and by prohibiting the deposit of funds in non-specie-paying banks.[1] A bill "for the more effective collection of the revenues in the lawful money of the United States" was therefore introduced,[2] authorizing the secretary to give notice that after December 31, 1816, revenues due the United States would be collected in specie, or in the notes of specie-paying banks,[3] and imposing a tax on the notes of non-specie-paying banks.[4]

This bill having failed of passage,[5] Webster introduced into the House of Representatives a set of resolutions, which he advocated on the ground that the prevailing practice constituted an infringement upon the constitutional prohibition that "no preference shall be given by any regulation of commerce or revenue to the ports of one state over those of another."[6]

These resolutions declared that: (1) All duties should be uniform, and no preference should be given to the ports of one state over those of another ; (2) the revenues of the United States should be collected in legal currency of the United States, treasury notes, and notes of the United States Bank ; (3) the secretary of the treasury should be required to carry these into effect.[7]

These were amended by dropping out the first declaration

---

[1] He also asked for a heavy tax on notes not redeemed in specie.—*Annals*, Fourteenth Cong., 1st Sess., p. 1229.

[2] By Calhoun.—*Ibid.*, pp. 1345–98.   [3] Sec. 1.   [4] Sec. 4.

[5] Because of the strength of the state-bank interests and the proposal to issue treasury notes to supply the deficiency.—*Ibid.*, p. 1405. See Sumner, *History of Banking, etc.*, p. 74.

[6] I, 9, 6.   [7] *Annals*, Fourteenth Cong., 1st Sess., p. 1440.

and by adding to the list of media receivable " the notes of specie-paying banks." [1]

The restriction of banks which did not redeem their notes in specie was to take effect February 20, 1817; but by that day the currency had been brought to a specie basis [2] all over the country; so that, by the resolutions, the mixed currency of state and national bank notes, treasury notes, and specie had been fastened on the treasury.

The charter of the Second Bank of the United States expired April 10, 1836. Already, in 1833, the public deposits had been removed from that bank; or, rather, after the 26th of September, 1833, all public moneys had been deposited with certain state banks. [3]

In view of the anticipated expiration of the charter of the

[1] This addition was proposed and then withdrawn by Calhoun in the House; and then added in the Senate.—*Ibid.*, pp. 1371, 1440, 1449.

The reason for proceeding by resolution instead of by bill is stated by Webster to be the fact that " the case is not one in which the law is deficient, but one in which the execution of the law is deficient." This resolution passed both houses of Congress on the 26th of April, 1816 ; was approved by the president on the 30th. Webster's description of the condition of affairs may be quoted : " The situation of the country with regard to finances and the collection of its revenues is most deplorable. With a perfectly sound legal currency, the national revenues are not collected in it, but in the paper of various sorts and degrees of value. Before the war the business of the country was conducted principally by means of the paper of the different state banks. As these were in good credit, and paid their notes in gold and silver, on demand, no great evil was experienced from the circulation of the paper. Not being, however, a part of the legal money of the country, it could not by law be received in the payment of duties, taxes, or other debts to the government. But being payable, and hitherto paid, on demand, the collectors and other agents of the government had generally received it as cash. It had been deposited as cash in the banks which received the deposits of government, and from them it had been drawn as cash, and paid off to creditors of the public. During the war this state of things changed. Many of the banks had been induced to make loans of a very great amount to the government. These loans were made by an issue of their own bills, which . . . . rested for redemption on government stocks. . . . . The excess of paper created alarm. Demands for payment began to be made on the banks and they all stopped payment. . . . . The depreciation is not uniform throughout the United States, but the notes are received in payment of taxes, etc. The result of this is that the people of the United States pay their duties and taxes in currency of different values in different places. . . . . Taxes collected in Massachusetts are one-quarter higher than those which are collected by virtue of the same laws in the District of Columbia."— *Writings*, Vol. III, p. 49; *Statutes at Large*, Vol. III, p. 343.

[2] SUMNER, *History of Banking, etc.*, p. 76.

[3] By November 1, 1836, eighty-eight state banks in twenty-four states, with a capital of $77,576,449, held public deposits amounting to $49,377,986.—*Ibid.*, p. 218.

federal bank, local banks multiplied rapidly,[1] used the public deposits as a basis for circulation, and so caused great inflation of the circulating medium.[2]

It was a period of great speculative activity, the public land being one of the chief subjects of such speculation. Receivability at the public land office became the test of the credit of a bank bill, and banks were organized for the purpose of issuing notes which might be used in payments in this way.[3]

On June 10, 1836, Benton introduced a bill in the Senate providing that bank notes and paper currency should cease to be receivable or offered in payment on account of the United States or of the post-office, or in fees of courts of the United States; those of less than $20, after March 3, 1837; less than $50, after March 3, 1838; those less than $100, after March 3, 1839; less than $500, after March 30, 1840; less than $1,000, after March 3, 1841; and all, after March 3, 1842.[4]

This bill got no farther than the second reading, and, in view of the situation in regard to the sale of public lands and the refusal of Congress to act, President Jackson had his secretary of the treasury (Woodbury) issue the famous Treasury Circular,[5] directed to receivers of public money and to the deposit banks, and ordering them to receive only specie,[6] " " in consequence of complaints which have been made

[1] SUMNER, *History of Banking, etc.*, p. 231. Between 1832 and 1837, three hundred and forty banks, with a capital of over $99,000,000, were organized.

[2] *Ibid.*, p. 219.

[3] If the bank failed, of course the treasury bore the loss.—See KNOX, *History of Banking in the United States*, pp. 80 f.

[4] *Debates of Congress*, Vol. XII, pt. II, p. 1745.

[5] July 11, 1836. This document can be found in *Senate Documents* 1836-7, No. 2, p. 416; or in DUNBAR, *Laws of the United States Relating to Currency, Finance, and Banking* (revised edition), p. 270. For an account of the political aspects of this act, see BENTON, *Thirty Years' View*, Vol. I, p. 676.

[6] With certain exceptions and indulgences in favor of *bona fide* settlers or residents of the state in which the land lay. It was claimed by the president that his action was authorized by the resolutions of 1816, which in giving the secretary power to receive gave him power to reject the notes of banks which claimed to be specie-paying institutions; *i. e.*, to judge whether or not they came within the category.

of frauds, speculations, and monopolies in the purchase of the public lands, and the aid which is said to be given to effect these objects by excessive bank credits," etc.

This action of the executive aroused intense feeling, and was the subject of immediate action on the part of Congress. On December 13 resolutions were introduced in the Senate with the intent of rescinding the circular,[1] and a discussion was begun involving the whole currency question.[2]

On January 26, 1837,[3] a bill was introduced providing that revenue should be receivable in the legal currency of the United States, in notes of banks, which were payable on demand in specie, if they were of denominations not lower than $5, after December 30, 1839; than $10 after December 30, 1840; or than $20 after December 30, 1841. This passed the Senate on February 10, 1837,[4] and the House on March 1,[5] but, being left unsigned by the president, it did not become a law.[6] The following year a resolution was adopted by the two houses of Congress to the effect that it should "not be lawful for the secretary of the treasury to make or continue in force any general order which shall create any difference between the different branches of the revenue as to the money or medium in which debts or dues accruing to the United States may be paid."[7]

The situation, then, was this: Gold and silver coin were of course a full legal tender and receivable for all public

[1] *Debates of Congress*, Vol. XIII, pt. I, p. 8.

[2] This debate turns largely on the true import of the resolutions of 1816. The circular was attacked on the ground that it was illegal as contravening those resolutions; that it was unconstitutional as discriminating between the citizens of different states; and evil in its effects on business and industry. It was in this debate December 21, 1813, that Webster spoke the oft-quoted words, "Most unquestionably there is no legal tender and there can be no legal tender in this country under the authority of the government other than gold and silver."—*Ibid.*, p. 93.

[3] *Ibid.*, p. 578.   [4] *Ibid.*, p. 778.

[5] *Ibid.*, pt. II, p. 2090.—This bill is found in DUNBAR'S *Laws*, p. 271.

[6] May 2, 1838, Clay introduced a bill substantially the same in effect.—*Globe*, Twenty-fifth Congress, 2d Sess., Appendix, p. 244.

[7] *Statutes at Large*, Vol. V, p. 310.

obligations; there were treasury notes out, likewise receivable for public dues;[1] by the resolution of 1816, all other media were prohibited than treasury notes, specie, and the notes of specie-paying banks;[2] by the treasury circular and the executive order only specie was to be accepted in payment for public lands; by the resolution of 1838 there was to be no discrimination between different kinds of revenue. The executive claimed that the effect of the resolutions of 1816 was to give discretion in accepting or rejecting the notes of banks in determining whether or not they came within the terms of the resolution; the banks claimed the right to have their notes employed in meeting obligations to the federal government, *i. e.*, the right to determine for themselves and the government whether or not they came within the description.

Congress and the executive finally agreed, in 1840, upon a gradual abrogation of the resolution,[3] as follows: After June 30, 1840, one-fourth of all payments to the federal government should be made in "the legal currency of the United States;" one-half after June 30, 1841; three-fourths after the same date in 1842; and, after June 30, 1843, the entire revenue should be so collected in that currency, which is explained to be gold and silver only. The next year this act was repealed;[4] but a few years later, when the independent treasury system was permanently established,[5] it was enacted that payments to the government and payments by the government should be only in gold and silver coin or in treasury notes issued under the authority of the United States.[6]

[1] See above, p. 106.

[2] The receivability of national-bank notes had been taken away by legislation; above, p. 139.

[3] The creation later of the independent treasury system brought about the divorce of treasury and banks.—*Statutes at Large*, Vol. V, p. 385, sec. 19.

[4] *Ibid.*, p. 439.   [5] August 6, 1846.—*Ibid.*, Vol. IX, p. 59, sec. 19.

[6] Treasury notes were to be issued by the government only with the consent of the creditor receiving them.

CHAPTER XII

CONCLUSION

If, in conclusion, the questions with which the inquiry began be called to mind they can be briefly answered with reference to the United States.

As to the agent of state through whom the power has been exercised, it may be said that in the colonies it was exercised by the colonial governments subject to the regulations and prohibition of Parliament.[1] Under the continental régime the power was exercised only by the states. Under the constitution such power as was believed to be vested in either government was bestowed upon the federal government as distinguished from that of the respective states; and prior to 1862 it was supposed that the power to bestow this quality on bills of credit was witheld from both. That power is now conceded to be likewise vested in Congress.

The objects on which the quality has been bestowed have been various: Crude substitutes for coin in the form of articles of use or ornament; coin, domestic and foreign; notes issued by the government, varying in character from true exchequer bills to bills adapted in all respects to monetary purposes; notes issued by institutions chartered under federal law; and, finally, notes issued by institutions owing their existence to commonwealth legislatures.

Nor are the reasons which have guided action difficult to state. They have been four in number: (1) The desire to give certainty to contracts drawn in terms of money units was

---

[1] Parliament could forbid that bills of credit should be made a tender; it could probably have named terms on which they might be made a tender, but the act of the local legislature would have been necessary to supplement this.

153

the object of such legislation as that of 1792. (2) To furnish to certain notes a partial redemption or to anticipate expected revenues was the object of such provisions as those characteristic of the treasury-note legislation prior to 1862. (3) To obtain a medium for the payment of obligations to and by the government was the purpose of receiving the state-bank notes in the years following 1814. (4) Finally, the hope of sustaining the value of the object upon which the quality was bestowed led to the legal-tender legislation of the war and the silver legislation of 1878.

Of these controlling motives the first may be said to be legal in its character, and not only legitimate, but essential to the proper relations of certainty between debtor and creditor. The economic question as to the proper nature of such legislation, whether the quality of being a tender should be bestowed upon all forms of money legitimized, or upon the one form only which is adopted as the standard of value, cannot be considered in such a study as this, purposely limited to the consideration of the political and constitutional aspects of the subject. It is hoped that the presentation of these particular phases of the problem of the attitude of the state towards its money may throw light upon others without the limits of this investigation.

The remaining motives named were monetary and financial, and, if within the competence of the government, should be judged by economic standards and by those considerations of public honesty and of expediency which should control the operations of a powerful government "founded on law."

The operations of the federal government in connection with the treasury notes prior to 1862 and with the state-bank notes may be classed with those of the English government, which were said to be due to "mistaken policy." They resulted from the confusion existing in the minds of those in control as to the distinction between monetary and fiscal operations, and the effort to make the former serve the latter purpose. In neither of these cases was the private individual injured in his rights or property, except in so far as a failure to perform what has long been considered a governmental function and supply a stable currency might be held to injure the individual.

In the case of the legal-tender notes, however, the result was different. Then, the private individual, the creditor, was by a compulsory act of government, through the agency of the courts established to work justice between man and man, forced to share with the government, or bear for it, the cost of the conflict then being waged. By an extraordinary departure from both legislative and judicial precedents an act as tyrannical as any act of Henry VIII. in dealing with his coins found legislative and executive support and judicial sanction. It was fitting that the law based on the doctrine of the prerogative prevailing in the time of the Tudors should be invoked to sustain such legislation.

APPENDICES

APPENDIX I

New York.—The legislation of February 25, 1862, came before the New York court of appeals in 1863 in two agreed cases, which became the leading cases on the subject until the Supreme Court of the United States passed upon the act.[1] In these cases the question of specie contracts did not arise;[2] simply the question of constitutionality of the act as regarded contracts drawn in general terms of "dollars" and "cents," or "lawful money of the United States." The court, by a vote of six to two,[3] upheld the act, the judges giving their opinion *seriatim.* Those who constituted the majority rested their conclusions on various grounds: The sovereign power over the money of the country was claimed for congress; the powers to regulate commerce, to borrow money, to raise and maintain armies, were in turn appealed to. The chief justice based his dissent on the power claimed for the states to regulate and control contracts, limited only by the constitutional prohibition.

State courts agreeing with New York.—The New York decision was followed by the courts of Iowa,[4] Wisconsin,[5] California,[6] New Hampshire,[7] Michigan,[8] Missouri,[9] Pennsylvania,[10] Vermont,[11] Tennessee,[12] South Carolina,[13] and Illinois.[14]

---

[1] Meyer *v.* Roosevelt, and Metropolitan and Shoe & Leather Bank *v.* Van Dyke, 27 N. Y. 400.

[2] The New York court likewise ruled that the act applied to contracts of this character, a decision overruled in Bronson *v.* Rodes.

[3] The opinion of Davies, J., is that quoted and referred to as authority by the courts of other states; the chief justice, Denio, was of the minority.

[4] Hintrager *v.* Bates, 18 Iowa. 174 (December, 1864). See also 16 Iowa, 243, 415.

[5] Breitenbach *v.* Turner, 18 Wis. 140 (1864).

[6] Lick *v.* Faulkner, 25 Cal. 404 (1864).   [7] George *v.* Conrad, 45 N. H. 434 (1864).

[8] Van Hoesen *v.* Kanourse, 13 Mich. 303 (1865).

[9] Riddlebarger *et al. v.* McDaniel, 38 Mo. 138. See 194, 458 (1866).

[10] Legal Tender Cases, 52 Pa. St. 9 (1866). Justice Strong participated in the decision of these cases.

[11] Carpenter *v.* Northfield Bank, 35 Vt. 46 (1866).

[12] Johnson *v.* Ivry, 4 Caldwell, 608 (1867).

[13] O'Neil *v.* McKern, 1 S. C. 147 (1869).   [14] Black *v.* Lusk, 69 Ill. 70 (1873).

State courts rejecting the New York precedent.—The courts of Kentucky and New Jersey refused to follow in this direction, and both held the act to be unconstitutional. The Kentucky decision[1] was upheld in the case of Hepburn *v.* Griswold, and need not be further treated. The New Jersey court had the question to face after the decision of Hepburn *v.* Griswold, but also after there was reason to believe that the Supreme Court would reopen the matter, and therefore argued upon the merits of the case.[2]

State courts taking middle ground.—The courts of Indiana and Georgia took middle ground, declaring that while the act was believed to be an excess of power, and so unconstitutional, because their decision was not a final one, but would be reviewed, they would resolve all doubts in favor of the act.[3]

APPENDIX II

SPECIE CONTRACTS

Doctrine of specific performance.—As the decision of Bronson *v.* Rodes depends upon the legal doctrine of specific performance, a word of explanation may be in place.

From very early times the courts of the common law have given in cases of breach of contracts a remedy in the form of money damages, and not in the form of enforced performance of the terms of the agreement, *i. e.*, not its specific performance.[4] As early as the fifteenth century, however, it was recognized that in many cases such procedure was wholly inadequate and resulted in a failure of justice, and the lord chancellor, who, as "keeper of the king's conscience," exercised an extraordinary jurisdiction, granted relief in the form of specific performance of the terms of the contract. Usually land, "real property," was the subject of contracts so inforced, because of the theory that in a breach of an agreement relating to personal property or chattels a money equivalent could always be found. And, until quite recent times, the court of equity would not act unless it could be shown that there was no remedy at law, or that such remedy as existed was wholly

---

[1] Griswold *v.* Hepburn, 2 Duval, 20 (1865).

[2] Martin's Ex'rs *v.* Martin *et al.*, 20 N. J. Eq. 421 (1870).

[3] Reynolds *v.* Bank of Indiana, 18 Ind. 462 (1862) ; also Thayer *v.* Hedges, 22 Ind. 282 (1864) ; Jones *v.* Harker, 37 Ga. 503 (1867).

[4] But see POLLOCK AND MAITLAND, *op. cit.*, Vol. II, p. 521.

inadequate. Lately, and particularly in the United States,[1] the attitude of the courts has been more liberal, and specific performance has come to be recognized as a suitable remedy in cases of breach of contracts having for their subject personal property or services, and in cases where there exists a remedy at law but that remedy is less effective in securing justice as between the parties.

Application to act of February 25, 1862.—As the text states,[2] when the act of February 25, 1862, was passed and the legal-tender notes were issued, one of the questions raised was whether or not the act applied to contracts expressed not simply in terms of dollars and cents, but in terms of dollars and cents followed by descriptive language showing a special case, or a special need, or implying that the word "dollars" was used rather to indicate weight and fineness than simple money units, such as "lawful silver money of the United States, each dollar weighing *at least* seventeen pennyweights and six grains,"[3] "dollars in gold,"[4] "dollars in gold and silver coin, lawful money of the United States."[5]

It is unnecessary to cite decisions of commonwealth courts other than the Pennsylvania cases, to which reference is made for illustration.   The question was generally held to be decided by the act of February 25, 1862, and these contracts held to be embraced within the terms of that act, together with contracts simply in terms of "lawful money."

Action of California and Nevada.— But in California and Nevada, where there was a strong feeling against the introduction of the legal-tender notes, legislation was enacted expressly granting a remedy in the form of specific performance in actions on such contracts, viz.: " In an action on a contract or obligation in writing for the direct payment in money made payable in a specified kind of money or currency, judgment for the plaintiff, whether the same be by default or after verdict, may follow the contract or obligation and be made payable in the kind of money or currency specified therein; and in an action against any person for the recovery of money received by such person in a fiduciary capacity or to the use of

[1] Story, *Equity Jurisprudence*, §§ 717 f.

[2] Above, p. 126.— See 29 Law. Rep. Ann., 412, note on " Special Contracts and Obligations to make Payment in Gold or Silver."

[3] Meroe *v.* Sailor, 52 Pa. St. 9.

[4] Laughlin *v.* Harvey, *Ibid.*, 9.

[5] Bronson *v.* Rodes, 7 Wallace, 229.

another, judgment for the plaintiff . . . . may be for the same kind of money or currency so received by such person." [1] An act in identical terms passed the Nevada legislature and became a law the following winter.[2] In both states this legislation was attacked because of its alleged unconstitutionality, as in conflict with the federal legal-tender act. In California the commonwealth act was upheld,[3] on the ground, first, that the act granted no new right, but simply provided a remedy where there had been none before, and, second, that Congress, by requiring the payment of import duties in coin, had shown that contracts for coin were not included in the terms of the act.[4]

The Nevada act had a more adventurous history. It was first declared void.[5] This decision was, however, three years later, reconsidered and reversed,[6] and the court declared that the former decision had never been observed by the honest and respectable portion of the community. The reasoning of the California court was then adopted.

Bronson v. Rodes.— In the same year the question came before the Supreme Court in Bronson v. Rodes,[7] and the California doctrine was upheld. This decision did away with the supposed necessity of such legislation, as was afterwards recognized by the Nevada court,[8] when it was decided that a contract made payable in "gold coin or its equivalent in United States legal-tender notes" could be enforced according to its terms even when there was no such legislation. The result of the decision in Bronson v. Rodes retains for the parties to a contract the right to elect between the two kinds of currency resulting from the legal-tender legislation, *i. e.*, between coin and paper.

The principle here laid down has found legislative sanction as between the two forms of metallic money, in the words of the act of

[1] *Session Laws of California*, 1863, chap. 421, sec. 2. The date of this act is April 27, 1863. See also *Codes of California, Annotated;* POMEROY, *Civil Procedure* (1901), sec. 667. This has been followed in some other states. See *Idaho Code Civil Procedure*, 1901, sec. 3506.

[2] January 4, 1864.   [3] Carpenter v. Atherton, 25 Cal. 564 (July, 1864).

[4] The ground taken in Bronson v. Rodes. This right was recognized also in the act of March 17, 1862, recognizing contracts for coin.— *Statutes at Large*, Vol. XII, p. 370. And of March 3, 1863, imposing a stamp duty in such contracts.—*Ibid.*, p. 713, sec. 4.

[5] Milleau v. Stout, 1 Nev. 573 (1865).   [6] Senn v. Minor, 4 Nev. 462 (1868).

[7] From New York, where the court had taken the other view.—7 Wallace, 229.

[8] Wells, Fargo & Co. v. Van Sickle, 6 Nev. 45 (1870).

1878, "unless otherwise expressly stated in the contract." But in several commonwealths the right of the individual to designate the form of money in which he shall be paid has been expressly limited.[1] And the Democratic Platform of 1896 advocated federal legislation doing away with this right.[2] "We favor such legislation as will prevent for the future the demonitization of any kind of legal-tender money by private contract."

APPENDIX III

DOCUMENTS CONNECTED WITH THE REHEARING OF THE LEGAL-TENDER QUESTION

WHEN the order for rehearing in the Legal-Tender Cases was entered, Chief Justice Chase is said to have accompanied it with a memorandum in which the proceedings of the court were described in such a fashion as to betray the confidences of the conference room and reflect on the honor of those justices who constituted a majority of the court. When the existence of this document was learned, a "Statement of Facts" was prepared by Justice Miller, and signed by the four justices agreeing with him, to be filed as a reply to the memorandum. It is said that the memorandum was then withdrawn, and the reply consequently not filed.

The memorandum of Chief Justice Chase is said to have been filed and then withdrawn; but whether it was filed and withdrawn or simply prepared and withheld does not appear with certainty. There is no minute concerning it upon the records of the Supreme Court. Neither Professor Hart, of Harvard University, the latest biographer of Mr. Chase, nor Professor Bourne, of Yale, now engaged in editing certain of the Chase papers, can give any information concerning the document, nor is it to be found among the papers of Mr. Chase now owned by the Congressional Library.[3] Something of its tenor may be ascertained from the following

---

[1] Kansas *Statutes of 1893*, chap. 99; *General Statutes* 1901, sec. 1200: ". . . . all obligations of debt . . . . stated in terms of dollars, and to be paid in money, if not dischargeable in United States legal tender notes, shall be payable in either the standard silver or gold coins authorized by the Congress of the United States, all stipulations in the contract to the contrary notwithstanding." *Session Laws of South Dakota*, 1891, chap. 85; also *Annotated Statutes*, 1901, sec. 4905, and CUTTING, *Compiled Laws of Nevada*, 1860–1900, sec. 2738.

[2] *Annual Encyclopædea*, 1896, p. 763.

[3] Professor Hart, Professor Bourne, Mr. Putnam, the librarian to Congress, and the clerk of the Supreme Court have been extremely courteous in replying to inquiries put to them concerning this interesting document.

extract from the dissenting opinion delivered by Mr. Chase in the second Legal Tender Case.[1]

A majority of the court, five to four, in the opinion which has just been read, reverses the judgment rendered by the former majority of five to three, in pursuance of an opinion formed after repeated arguments at successive terms and careful consideration; and declares the legal-tender clause to be constitutional. . . . . And this reversal, unprecedented in the history of the court, has been produced by no change in the opinion of those who concurred in the former judgment. One closed an honorable judicial career by resignation after the case had been decided (27 November, 1867), after the opinion had been read and agreed to in conference (29 January, 1870), and after the day when it would have been delivered in court (31 January, 1870) had not the delivery been postponed for a week to give time for the preparation of the dissenting opinion. The court was then full, but the vacancy caused by the resignation of Mr. Justice Grier having been subsequently filled, and an additional justice having been appointed under the act increasing the number of judges to nine, which took effect on the first Monday in December, 1869, the then majority find themselves in a minority of the court, as now constituted, upon the question. Their convictions, however, remain unchanged.

The "Statement of Facts" evoked by this Memorandum, which seems to have disappeared, has experienced a better fate. Passing from the widow of Justice Miller to Justice Bradley, it was kept under seal by him, and left with instructions that it should be published only when all the persons concerned in the great controversy has passed away. With the death of Justice Field this condition was fulfilled, and Mr. Charles Bradley,[2] the son of Justice Bradley, has therefore been able to include it in a volume recently published.[3]

This Statement of Facts is as follows:

Latham *v.* The United States.
Deming *v.* The United States.

The very singular paper filed by the Chief Justice in these cases, in regard to the order of the Court, by which they are set down for

[1] Knox *v.* Lee, etc., 12 Wallace, 572.

[2] I have the consent of Mr. Bradley to include the paper here, and wish to acknowledge my appreciation of his courtesy in granting me that permission.

[3] *Miscellaneous Writings of the Late Hon. Joseph P. Bradley, and a Review of His "Judicial Record," by William Draper Lewis and an Account of His "Dissenting Opinions," by the Late A. Q. Keasby, Esq., of Newark, N. J.*, edited and compiled by his son, Charles Bradley (Newark, N. J. L. J. Hardman, 1902).

hearing on all the questions presented by their respective records, leaves the court no alternative but to present a reply in the same manner that the statement of the Chief Justice was presented.

The paper itself is without precedent in the records of the Court. On the first day of this month the court announced, by the mouth of the Chief Justice, that these cases would be heard on the 11th day of the month, on all the issues involved in the record.

In making this announcement the Chief Justice did all that was necessary to prevent any misconception of his opinions by stating that he and Justices Nelson, Clifford and Field dissented from the order. This statement was placed in the records of the court.

The present statement [that of the chief justice], therefore, was not necessary to explain the position of those gentlemen, or to vindicate their action, for it was well understood and was assailed by no one.

It is an effort to take the action of the court out of the ordinary and usual rules which govern it in the simple matter of deciding when it will hear a case, and what shall be heard in that case, and subject the court to censure, because it will not consent to have the rights of the parties in such cases controlled by the vague recollection of some members of the Court, presented only in conference, not reduced to writing, nor ever submitted to the consideration of counsel charged with the conduct of the cases. If this be a just ground of censure, we must submit to it, and will be content to bear it.

In reference to the facts on which the Court acted, it is conceded by all that the cases, having been passed without losing their place on the docket, were entitled to a preference whenever either party should call them up and insist on a hearing. The attorney general, on behalf of the United States, did this on Friday, March 25. At the same time he stated that the cases presented the same question in regard to the constitutionality of the legal tender statutes that had been decided in the case of Hepburn *v.* Griswold, at the present term, and asked the court to hear argument on that question. Mr. Carlisle, counsel for Latham, was present, and reminded the court that some six weeks before he had asked that his case might be set down for hearing, and that he now wished for an early hearing, but hoped that the legal tender question would not be reconsidered in his case.

He did not at that time intimate in any manner that there had been any agreement of counsel, or any action of the Court, which precluded that question in his case.

The next day being conference day, the Court acted on the motion of the Attorney General; but on Monday morning, before it could be announced, the Chief Justice produced a letter from Mr. Carlisle to him, remonstrating against reopening the legal tender question in his case, and insisting that he had a right to expect that the case of

Hepburn *v.* Griswold would, as to that point, decide his case also; but he did not state in that letter that any order had been made to that effect, or any agreement of counsel, verbal or otherwise.

This letter of Mr. Carlisle, the only written document, paper or statement ever presented to the Court before its order was announced, as a foundation for refusing to hear the legal tender question in the two cases, was never filed with the clerk, and cannot now be found by us.

The Court, in deference to Mr. Carlisle's statement, made an order that on Thursday, the 31st of March, the whole matter should be heard in open court. On that day the Attorney General, who had been shown Mr. Carlisle's letter, appeared and insisted on his motion. Mr. Carlisle opposed it, and in argument gave his history of the cases in this court. He also argued that from that history he had a right to expect that whatever should be the judgment of the court in *Hepburn* v. *Griswold* as to the constitutionality of the legal tender acts, should conclude that matter in his case. *But he did not state or rely on any agreement with counsel of the Government of the one case by the other, or any express order of the court to that effect.*

Mr. Merriman, the senior counsel in Deming's case, was present at this argument. He took no part in it. He made no objection to the argument of the legal tender question in his case, and did not then claim, nor has he ever claimed in court, that that question was precluded by any action of the Court or agreement of counsel.

On full consideration of all that was then before it, the Court announced on Friday morning, the first of April, that the two cases would be heard on all the questions presented by the records on Monday, the 11th, ten days thereafter; and at the same time the chief justice announced the dissent of himself and the other justices already mentioned to this order.

When that day arrived, a letter was presented from Mr. Carlisle, dated in this city, of the Saturday before, in which he said he had not had time to prepare for the argument, and that he had an engagement to try a case in New York on Tuesday, which he had not been able to postpone, and again urged the injustice of a reargument of the legal tender question in his case, and stated that he understood when his case had been passed that *it would abide the decision in Hepburn* v. *Griswold.* A telegram was also read stating Mr. Merriman's illness. The Court from the bench postponed the hearing for one week.

Since that time the Chief Justice has received a letter from Mr. Norton, former solicitor of the Court of Claims, who once had some charge in that capacity of these cases, in which he states that when the cases were continued in March, 1868, he understood that they would be governed as to the legal tender question by the decision of *Hepburn*

v. *Griswold.* Of both these letters, now the only papers on file in regard to the matter, it is to be observed —

1. That they were presented after the Court had appointed a day for hearing all that might be said for or against the motion, and after both parties had had a full hearing and after the Court had, on full consideration of all that was before it, fixed the day for hearing and decided to hear the whole matter in issue. Of Mr. Norton's letter it may be further said, that it was made after Mr. Carlisle's two efforts to prevent a hearing had both been considered and overruled, and is made by a gentleman not now engaged in the cases, without verification, and without notice to any party, or counsel in the case.

2. That neither of them asserts that any agreement, contract or promise was made by the counsel of the United States that *Hepburn* v. *Griswold* could control these cases in any matter of law whatever.

We do not doubt that counsel for appellants and counsel for the United States believed, and in that sense understood, that the judgment of the Supreme Court in Hepburn vs. Griswold, and the other legal tender cases argued at the same time, would establish principles on that subject that would govern the cases now under consideration, and all other cases in which the same questions might arise.

This understanding was no more than the expectation, usual and generally well founded, that a principle decided by this court will govern all cases falling within it. But this expectation must be subordinated to the possibility, fortunately rare, that the Court may reconsider the questions so decided; and confers no absolute right.

We have thus far considered only what occurred in open court since the motion of the attorney general was made to take up these cases; and in what has been said the court, consisting of Justices Swayne, Miller, Davis, Strong and Bradley, all concur. But the paper, to which we are replying, undertakes to give a history of the connection of these two cases with certain others, involving the legal tender question, so much at variance with the records of the Court and with the recollections of the three Justices of the Court first above named (the other two not then being members of the court), that we do not feel at liberty to permit it to pass in silence.

This statement invades the sanctity of the conference room, and, in support of its assault upon the court, does not hesitate to make assertions which are but feebly supported by the recollections of a part of the four judges who joined in it, but which are inconsistent with the record of the court, and are contradicted by the clearest recollections of the other three judges who then composed a part of the Court, who join in this answer:

It is attempted, by speaking of these cases as two out of nine, which the court constantly had in view as involving the legal tender question, to sustain the inference, that they were to be decided with the others, and were submitted to the Court, so far as the legal tender question was concerned, at the same time. Now, the first and only time the legal tender cases were grouped together in any order of the court was on the second day of March, 1868, when the following order was made of record:

"No. 89. S. P. & H. P. Hepburn v. Henry Griswold.

"No. 225. Frederick Bronson v. Peter Rodes.

"Ordered by the Court, that these cases stand continued for reargument by counsel at bar on the first Tuesday of the next term and that the Attorney General have leave to be heard on the part of the United States."

"No. 35. Mandelbaum v. People of Nevada.

"No. 60. The County of v. the State of Oregon.

"No. 67. John A. McGlynn, Ex'r., etc., v. Emily Magraw, Ex'trix.

"No. 71. Joseph C. Willard v. Benj. O. Tayloe.

"Ordered by the Court, that these causes stand continued to the next term, with leave to counsel to reargue the same if they see fit on any question common to them and to Nos. 89 and 225."

The Chief Justice says that there were nine of these cases in all, which were to be governed by the decision of the Court made on the general argument in regard to legal tender. Here are six of them grouped in these two entries standing together. If Latham's and Deming's cases stood on the same agreement or the same order, why were they not included ? It will not do to say that they were carelessly omitted, for the order is evidently drawn with particularity, and there can be no doubt that it includes all that it was intended to include.

Nor will it do to say that these cases could not be included because they had other questions besides legal tender, for the cases of *Willard* v. *Tayloe* and *Mandelbaum* v. *Nevada*, which are in the order, included other questions, and were finally decided without touching that question. The case of *Horwitz* v. *Butler*, which is necessary to make out the nine alluded to, although it involved nothing else but legal tender, was argued by itself after *Bronson* v. *Rodes* was decided. There was, therefore, evidently no general agreement or order that cases not named should abide those that were, because they involved that question.

It is said that subsequently to the decision of *Hepburn* v. *Griswold* these cases "were called on several occasions, and it was again stated by the Chief Justice from the bench that the legal tender question having been determined in the other cases, would not be again heard in these."

This statement is, as we are satisfied, founded in an entire misapprehension. If any statement had been made from the bench that no argument would be heard in these cases of the legal tender question, it would certainly have attracted the attention of the judges who did not agree to that opinion, and would have met with a denial on their part so emphatic as to be remembered.

The cases now under consideration were numbered six and seven of the docket of this term. They had, therefore, as the records of the courts show, been called and passed on the 8th December, two months before the announcement of the decision of *Hepburn* v. *Griswold*, which was Feb. 8.

It further appears, that on the 10th December the Attorney General moved to dismiss the appeal in Latham's case because it had not been taken in due time. The opinion of the Chief Justice is entered of record over-ruling this motion, because, though the appeal was not allowed within ninety days, it had been prayed within that time. In all these orders no hint is given that these cases were to abide the judgment in *Hepburn* v. *Griswold*.

Very soon after the decision of *Hepburn* v. *Griswold*, Mr. Carlisle called attention to the Latham case, and asked that an early day be assigned for its hearing. The Chief Justice was about to do this in open court when Mr. Justice Miller requested him to take the matter into conference. When the motion was called in conference, Mr. Justice Miller said that the case involved the legal tender question, and that he hoped it would not be set for hearing until the two vacancies on the bench were filled, as nominations were then pending for both of them. No objection was made to this, and the motion of Mr. Carlisle was postponed indefinitely. The Chief Justice remarked, as those of us who were present well recollect, that he considered the legal tender question as settled by *Hepburn* v. *Griswold*, as far as it went, but none of the judges gave any intimation that there was anything in the history of these which precluded that question from being considered in them. If it could not, there was no reason for postponing their hearing for a full bench, as was done, for they are otherwise quite unimportant, either in principle or amount, and were entitled to a speedy hearing, as they had been long delayed.

Conceding, as we do freely, that our brethren believed that such an order or statement was made verbally, should it govern our action?

We cannot consent to this, because if any order or statement was made orally, unless it was reduced to record or is assented to or admited by the counsel for the United States, it is no sufficient legal ground for refusing to hear the appellee on any defence found in the record of these cases.

In support of this we hold the law to be that without some order of Court made of record, or some written stipulation signed by the party or his counsel, or some verbal agreement of the parties established to the satisfaction of the Court, no party can be deprived of the right to any defence in this court which the record of his case presents.

Much stress is laid in the paper we are considering upon the long deliberation, the clear majority and the liberality of the court in giving time to the minority to file the dissent in *Hepburn* v. *Griswold,* and we are freely told the steps in conference which led to the final result.

The minority in that case are profoundly impressed with the belief that the circumstances of that decision, if well understood, would deprive it of the weight usually due to the decisions of this Court. The cases had been on hand eighteen months or more. There was no pressure for a decision. There was one vacancy on the bench. It was believed that there would soon be another. Under these circumstances the minority begged hard for delay until the bench was full. But it was denied. When, after all this argument and protracted consideration, the case was taken up in conference, and was there discussed for three or four hours, in which discussion every judge took part, the vote was taken and the court was found to be equally divided on affirming or reversing the judgment of the Court of Appeals of Kentucky.*

Before the conference closed, however, the vote of one of the judges who had been for reversing the judgment was changed. The circumstances under which this vote was changed were very significant, but we do not deem it proper to state them here. Without that change no opinion could have been rendered holding the legal tender statutes unconstitutional.

The question thus decided is of immense importance to the government, to individuals and to the public. The decision only partially disposed of the great question to which it related, and has not been received by the profession or by the public as conclusive of the matter. If it is ever to be reconsidered, a thing which we deem inevitable, the true interests of all demands that it be done at the earliest practicable moment.

We did not seek the occasion, but when the case seemed fairly before us we could not shrink from our duty as we understood it.

We could not deny to a party in Court the right which the law gave him to a hearing on all the defences which he claimed to have. When, on the other hand, the rules of the court did not admit of a rehearing in the case of *Hepburn* v. *Griswold,* we did not attempt to strain or modify those rules to reach the question. In this case, as in all others, we have endeavored to act as the law and our duty required.

The foregoing paper of eighteen pages was prepared and agreed to as the reply of the court to a paper filed by the Chief Justice on behalf of himself and Justices Nelson, Clifford and Field. That paper has been withdrawn by him from the files of the court, and this is, therefore, not filed.

We all concur in the statement of the foregoing paper as to the reasons for our action in the matter to which it refers, and the statement of facts we declare to be true so far as they are matters which took place while we were respectively members of the Supreme Court.

N. H. SWAYNE,
SAM F. MILLER,
DAVID DAVIS,
W. STRONG,
JOSEPH P. BRADLEY.

WASHINGTON, April 30, 1870.

[NOTE.— The original draft of the statement as drawn by Justice Miller from the asterisk on p. 167, concluded in the words printed below; but on consultation with the other justices at the time it was thought best to omit it, as Justice Grier was still living, and might be pained if it should come to his knowledge. Justice Miller, however, preserved it, and placed it in the same envelope with the statement as modified, where it was found after his death. It was as follows:]

This would have affirmed the judgment, but settled no principle.

An attempt was then made to convince an aged and infirm member of the court that he had not understood the question on which he voted. He said that he understood the Court of Appeals of Kentucky had declared the legal tender law unconstitutional, and he voted to reverse that judgment. As this was true, the case of *Hepburn* v. *Griswold* was declared to be affirmed by a court equally divided, and we passed to the next case.

This was the case of *McGlynn*, Ex., v. *Magraw*, and involved another aspect of the legal tender question. In this case the venerable Judge referred to, for whose public services and character we entertain the highest respect, made some remarks. He was told that they were inconsistent with his vote in the former case. He was reminded that he had agreed with a certain member of the Court in conversation on propositions differing from all the other judges, and finally his vote was obtained for affirming *Hepburn* v. *Griswold;* and so the majority, whose judgment is now said to be so sacred, was obtained.

To all this we submitted. We could do nothing else. In a week from that day every Judge on the bench authorized a committee of their number to say to the Judge who reconsidered his vote that it was their unanimous opinion that he ought to resign.

These are the facts. We make no comment. We do not say he did not agree to the opinion. We only ask: Of what value was his concurrence, and of what value is the judgment under such circumstances?

That question thus decided is of immense importance to the Government, to the public and to individuals. The decision only partly disposed of the great question to which it related, and has not been received by the profession or by the public as concluding the matter. If it is ever to be reconsidered, a thing which we deem inevitable, the best interests of all concerned, public and private, demand that it be done at the earliest practicable moment.

We have not sought the occasion, but when the case is fairly before us, if it shall be found to be so in these cases, we shall not shrink from our duty, whatever that may be. For the present, we believe it is our duty to hear argument on this question in these cases. Whether the judgment of the court in *Hepburn* v. *Griswold* shall be found by the court to be conclusive, or whether its principles shall be reconsidered and reversed, can only be known after the hearing; and in the final judgment of the Court, whatever it may be, we are satisfied there will be acquiescence.

At all events, the duty is one which we have not sought — which we cannot avoid.

APPENDIX IV

CONTROVERSY PROVOKED BY THE PROPOSITION TO ORGANIZE A BANK UNDER FEDERAL LAW

THE bill providing for the creation of a bank of the United States provoked long discussion in the House because of its alleged unconstitutionality, but was carried on February 8, 1791, by a vote of 39 to 20.[1] It had passed the Senate January 20.[2] When presented to the president he sought the advice of his attorney general, Edmund Randolph, his secretary of state, Jefferson, and his secretary of the Treasury, Hamilton. The two former argued against its constitutionality, as Madison had done in the debate in the House.

The Continental Congress had chartered the Bank of North America on December 31, 1781. There was a question as to its constitutionality, and the states were requested to provide that there should be no other bank during the war.[3] By article XII of the plan submitted by Robert Morris in 1781, for a bank, and approved by Congress, it was provided that "the bank notes payable on demand shall by law be made receivable in the duties and taxes of every state in the Union, and from the respective states by the treasury of the United States as specie."[4]

---

[1] *Annals of Congress*, Vol. I, p. 1960.　　　[2] *Ibid.*, Vol. I, p. 1748.

[3] *Journals of Congress*, Vol. VII, pp. 108, 256.

[4] Submitted to Congress May 17, 1781.—*Journals of Congress*, Vol. VII, p. 108.

Hamilton's argument in favor of such an institution is of especial interest, being the substance of the argument of the court in the case of McCulloch *v.* Maryland, in which, in 1819, the doctrine of implied powers was laid down. The use of this case later in the Legal-Tender Cases gives it again a peculiar significance.

The president was persuaded by the arguments of Hamilton and signed the bill.

ARGUMENTS ADVANCED

In congress. — Madison's argument was to the following effect:[1] The grant of powers to the federal government is a grant of particular powers. If this power is granted, it is a constructive (*i. e.,* implied according to the usage), not an express, power. The nearness or remoteness to the express power should be considered ("its incidentality"). This power, if granted, would be incidental to one of the three clauses giving power (1) to borrow money; (2) to lay and collect taxes to pay the debts, etc.; (3) to pass laws necessary and proper, etc. He finds that it is not incident to either of the first two. As to the third, no interpretation of that must be given which gives Congress unlimited discretion. The meaning of that clause should be "limited to means necessary to the end and incident to the nature of the specified powers."

To borrow money is made the end, and the accumulation of capital implied as the means; the accumulation of capital is then made the end and a bank implied as the means; the bank is then the end, and a charter of incorporation, a monopoly, capital punishments, etc., implied as the means. If implication, thus remote and thus multiplied, can be linked together, a chain may be formed that will reach every object of legislation.

A stricter rule of interpretation is to be found in the constitution when powers obviously incidental to other powers are yet expressly granted and not left to implication.

In addition to the arguments of Madison, Jackson, who claimed to have first called attention to the unconstitutional nature of the bill, urged its probable interference with state banks and its monopolistic character.[2]

On the other hand, it was urged[3] that Congress might do what was necessary to the end for which the constitution was adopted,

---

[1] February 2, *Annals of Congress*, Vol. I, p. 1899.

[2] *Annals of Congress*, Vol. I, p. 1917.   [3] By Ames and Sedgwick, *Ibid.*, p. 1910.

provided it is not repugnant to the natural rights of man, or to those which they have expressly reserved to themselves, or to the powers which they have assigned to the states.   Banks are considered by most governments indispensably necessary.   As to the power to create corporations, this may be derived from the power to hold property and make needful rules and regulations for its control.   One way of exercising such control would be through the agency of a corporation.

In the cabinet.— Summary of the argument of Randolph, February 12, 1791: The power to grant charters of incorporation is not expressly granted to Congress.   If it may be exercised, it is because the nature of the federal government allows it; or because it is involved in some of the specified powers of legislation; or because it is necessary and proper to carry into execution some of the specified powers.   (1) To rest the power on the first supposition would be to accept a method of interpretation so vague as to grasp every power; (2) to rest the power on one of the specified powers, under the strict method of interpretation which should be followed in a grant of limited powers, requires a close scrutiny of the powers to which it might be attached.   These are (*a*) the power of taxation, which, when analyzed, shows no need of the granting of corporate charters, being composed of the power to ascertain the subjects of taxation, the rate of taxation, the mode of collection, and to ordain the manner of accounting; (*b*) the power to borrow money, consisting of the power to stipulate the sum lent, the interest to be paid, and the time and manner of repayment, equally fails to show this as requisite; (*c*) the power to regulate commerce is similarly separated into parts and shown to be independent, in the view of the attorney-general, of the power to grant charters of incorporation; (*d*) the power to make rules and regulations respecting the territory or other property belonging to the United States and the preamble to the constitution are not found to show any necessity for the exercise of this power.

The clause "necessary and proper," while it should not be treated as restricting the powers of Congress, should not on the other hand be held to extend them; it should rather be treated "as among the surplusage which as often proceeds from inattention as from caution." [1]

---

[1] Clarke and Hall, *Legislative and Documentary History of the Bank of the United States* (1832), p. 86.

The argument of Jefferson, then secretary of state, leading to the same conclusion took the following form:

(*a*) The incorporation of the bank violated various state laws, *e. g.*, the laws of alienage; the laws governing descents; those of forfeiture and escheat; the laws of distribution; and those controlling monopoly.

(*b*) The controlling principle of interpretation must be found in the statement that "all powers not delegated to the United States by the constitution nor prohibited by it to the states are reserved to the states or to the people." [1]

(*c*) The power to grant charters is admittedly not expressly granted; it is not implied in power to lay taxes, to borrow money, or to regulate commerce; nor is it included in the power granted by the words "to provide for the general welfare," which simply indicates the purpose for which taxes may be laid; nor in the power "to make laws necessary and proper," since "necessary" means something other and less than simply "convenient;" *i. e.*, those means without which the grant of power would be nugatory.

The bank not being indispensably necessary, its incorporation is beyond the power of Congress.[2]

Hamilton argued as follows: [3]

(*a*) Every power vested in the government is in its nature sovereign, and includes by force of the term a right to employ all the means requisite and fairly applicable to the attainment of the ends of such power, and which are not precluded by restrictions and exceptions specified in the constitution, or not immoral, or not contrary to the essential ends of political society.

In the United States the federal government and the state governments are sovereign, each with regard to its proper objects.

The power to erect corporations is incident to sovereignty, and therefore belongs to the United States, in relation to the objects intrusted to that government.

(*b*) A distinction should be made as to "express powers," "implied powers," and "resulting powers," the latter two being delegated as fully as the express powers.

The power to incorporate in the case of conquered territory

---

[1] *Constitution of the United States*, Amendment X.

[2] *Jefferson's Writings*, Vol. V, p. 284; see Sumner, *History of Banking in the United States*, p. 48.

[3] *Hamilton's Writings* (edited by J. C. Hamilton, New York, 1851), Vol. IV, p. 104.

would be a power resulting from the nature of government; the power to incorporate to carry into effect a power expressly granted is an implied power. In both cases a power to incorporate exists.

(c) The word "necessary" in the constitution does not mean "indispensably" or "absolutely" necessary; but rather, "needful," "useful," "conducive to," etc. The policy of the government has already shown this to be the understanding.

(d) The rule laid down as to liberal interpretation of the state and strict construction by the federal constitution cannot hold, in view of the vaster and more complicated interests intrusted to the latter.

(e) As to the danger of abuse and intrusion into spheres of state activity, it is not to be so much dreaded as the cramping effect of the opposite interpretation.

(f) The criterion of necessity is (1) the end to be accomplished; (2) the question, does it abridge the right of any state or individual?

(g) The proposed bank will aid in the collection of taxes, by increasing the quantity of the circulating medium and quickening circulation, and thus increasing the means of payment; and by creating a convenient species of medium in which taxes can be paid. That is, Congress may name the medium in which taxes may be paid, and so may select bills issued under the authority of the United States. And as to manner of issuing such bills, discretion may be again exercised, and for this the creation of a bank may be selected as the best method.

Similarly with the regulation of commerce and the war power.

And, finally, it is within the power to regulate property belonging to the United States.

By the Supreme Court in the case of McCulloch v. The State of Maryland (1819), 4 Wheaton 316.—By an act of the Maryland legislature it was made penal for any bank or branch of a bank doing business in the state, without the authority of the state, "to issue notes in any manner, of any other denomination than five, ten, twenty, fifty, one hundred, five hundred, and one thousand dollars," and notes of these denominations were to be issued on stamped paper, for which they should pay the state treasurer certain fixed rates or an annual payment in advance of fifteen thousand dollars. For a violation of this act the officers were made personally and individually liable to the penalty of five hundred dollars each, and to recover such a penalty this suit was brought. The decision in the state courts was against the officials of the bank, and the cause was brought on writ of error to the Supreme Court.

The substance of the argument of interest here is as follows: The constitution derives its force, not from the states, but from the people, and creates a government which, though limited in its powers, is supreme within its sphere of action.

The power to create a corporation, though not an expressly granted power, may be implied. The great powers of taxation, borrowing money, regulating commerce, waging war, and maintaining armies and navies, being intrusted to the federal government, indicate that it is likewise intrusted with ample means for their execution.

Raising revenues and applying them to national purposes implies the power to convey money from one place to another, and of selecting an appropriate method of such conveyance.

It is true the creation of a corporation appertains to sovereignty; but not to one portion of sovereignty rather than another. Since the power of sovereignty is in the United States divided between the states and the federal government, the means necessary to carry these into effect belong to both. Moreover, the constitution has expressly granted the power to enact all laws "necessary and proper," which is not a cause of limitation, as is shown by its location ("among the powers granted") and by its purporting to grant an additional power. "Let the end be legitimate, let it be within the scope of the constitution, and all means which are appropriate, which are plainly adapted to that end, which are not prohibited, but consist with the letter and spirit of the constitution, are constitutional." A corporation is such a means, and the act creating the corporation of the bank is therefore constitutional.

BIBLIOGRAPHY

Anson, Sir W. R.   Law and Custom of the Constitution.   2d ed. 1892.

Ashley, W. J.   An Introduction to English Economic History and Theory.   The Middle Ages.   3d ed.   New York, 1898.

Bancroft, G.   A Plea for the Constitution Wounded in the House of its Guardians.   New York, 1886.

Barnett-Smith, G.   History of the English Parliament, together with an Account of the Parliaments of Scotland and Ireland. London, 1892.

Bolles, A. S.   The Financial History of the United States.   New York, 1879–86.

Breckenridge, R. M.   A Study of the Demand Notes of 1861. *Sound Currency*, Vol. V, No. 20.

Bronson, H.   Connecticut Currency.   Papers of New Haven Historical Society, No. 1.

Bullock, C. J.   Essays on the Monetary History of the United States.

Carlile, W. W.   The Evolution of Modern Money.   1901.

Cunningham, W.   The Growth of English Industry and Commerce during Early and Middle Ages.   3d ed.   Cambridge, 1896.

Davis, A. McF.   Currency and Banking in the Province of the Massachusetts Bay.   *Publications of the American Economic Association*, December, 1900.

Elliot's Debates in the Several State Conventions on the Adoption of the Federal Constitution.

Felt, J. B.   An Historical Account of Massachusetts Currency. Boston, 1839.

Frothingham, R.   The Rise of the Republic of the United States. 6th ed.

Green, J. R.   A History of the English People.   New York, 1881.

Hale, Sir Matthew.   The History of the Pleas of the Crown.   1st Amer. ed., Philadelphia, 1847.

Hallam, H.   A Constitutional History of England from the Accession of Henry VII. to the Death of George II.   5th ed.

Hare, J. I. C. American Constitutional Law. Boston, 1889.

Hart, A. B. Salmon Portland Chase. American Statesman Series.

Hickcox, J. H. A History of the Bills of Credit or paper money issued by New York from 1709 to 1789. Albany, 1866.

Hutchinson, T. The History of Massachusetts from the first settlement thereof in 1628 until the year 1750. 3d ed.

James, E. J. The Legal Tender Decisions. *Publications of the American Economic Association*, Vol. III.

Jefferson's Writings, edited by Paul Leicester Ford.

Kenyon, R. L Gold Coins of England. London, 1884.

Knox, J. J. A History of Banking in the United States. New York, 1900.

Knox, J. J. United States Notes. New York, 1885.

Laughlin, J. L. The History of Bimetallism in the United States. 4th ed.

Libby, O G. The Geographical Distribution of the Vote on the Federal Constitution.

Liverpool, Charles, 1st Earl of. A Treatise on the Coins of the Realm; in a Letter to the King. London, 1880.

Madox, T. The History and Antiquities of the Exchequer of the Kings of England. 2d ed. London, 1769.

Mommsen, T. History of Rome. Translated by W. P. Dickson. New York: Scribner, 1895.

Phillips, H. Historical Sketches of the Currency of the American Colonies prior to the adoption of the federal constitution.

Pollock and Maitland. History of the English Law before the Time of Edward I. Cambridge, 1895.

Potter, E. Some account of the bills of credit or paper money of Rhode Island from the first issue in 1710 to the final issue in 1786. *Rhode Island Historical Tracts*, No. 8.

Ripley, W. Z. Financial History of Virginia, 1609–1776.

Ruding, R. Annals of the Coinage of Britain and its dependencies from the earliest period of authentic history. London, 1817.

Schuckers, J. W. The Life and Public Services of Salmon Portland Chase. New York, 1874.

Spaulding, E. G. History of Legal Tender Paper Money. Buffalo, 1869.

Story, J. Commentaries on the Constitution of the United States. 5th ed. Boston, 1891.

Stubbs, W. Constitutional History of England in its Origin and Development. 5th ed. Oxford, 1891.

Stubbs, W. Select Charters and Other Illustrations of English Constitutional History from the Earliest Times to the Reign of Edward I. 8th ed. Oxford, 1890.

Sumner, W. G. The Finances and the Financier of the Revolution. New York, 1892.

Sumner, W. G. A History of Banking in the United States.

Taswell-Langmead, T. P. English Constitutional History from the Teutonic Conquest to the Present Time. 4th ed. London, 1890.

Thayer, J. B. Legal Tender. *Harvard Law Review*, Vol. I.

Tucker, J. R. The Constitution of the United States. Chicago, 1899.

United States Treasury Circular No. 123. Information respecting United States bonds, paper currency, etc. July 1, 1896.

Webster. The Works of Daniel Webster. Boston, 1851.

Weedon, W. B. Economic and Social History of New England, 1620–1789. Boston, 1891.

General reference is also made to public documents; for example, *Statutes at Large*, *Revised Statutes*, journals of legislative bodies, and court reports which have been available and found to be of service. The citations in the notes will prove an adequate guide in making use of these authorities.

INDEX

179